the
BROKE
Witch

**MAGICK SPELLS
AND POWERFUL
POTIONS THAT USE
WHAT YOU CAN
GROW, FIND, OR
ALREADY HAVE**

(DEBORAH CASTELLANO)

CASTLE POINT BOOKS
NEW YORK

www.castlepointbooks.com

The Castle Point Books trademark is owned by Castle Point Publishing, LLC.
Castle Point books are published and distributed by St. Martin's Publishing Group.

ISBN 978-1-250-28786-1 (paper over board)
ISBN 978-1-250-28814-1 (ebook)

Edited by Jennifer Calvert
Design by Melissa Gerber

Our books may be purchased in bulk for promotional, educational, or business use.
Please contact your local bookseller or the Macmillan Corporate and Premium Sales
Department at 1-800-221-7945, extension 5442, or by email at
MacmillanSpecialMarkets@macmillan.com.

First Edition: 2024

10 9 8 7 6 5 4 3 2 1

Mom,
you always let me read
whatever I wanted.
This one is for you.

CHAPTER 6

Divination DIY   *133*

CHAPTER 7

In Your Defense   *157*

CHAPTER 8

Modern Glamour Magick   *173*

CHAPTER 9

The Company You Keep   *189*

Practical Magick

AFTER CENTURIES OF DANCING (occasionally naked) on the outskirts of society, witchcraft and mysticism are all the rage today. Practitioners are social media phenoms and the protagonists of blockbuster stories. Magickal objects that used to be relegated to shadowy stores off the beaten path are now in display windows on Main Street. But at what cost?

From upmarket herb bundles and designer essential oils to pricey crystal towers and branded chakra candles, what was once a spiritual connection to the earth is now a not-so-subtle sign of the trendy (and spendy) witch. And that makes it easy to think you need All the Things™ to practice magick. While a witchy shopping spree can definitely be fun (who doesn't want a room full of shiny crystals?), the heart of witchcraft has very little to do with merch. It's all about finding a spiritual connection. And there are so many ways to do that without clicking on "add to cart."

The Broke Witch is the guide to spellcraft and connection the way it was intended to be practiced—with your mind, heart, and spirit, and not your credit card. Its lessons in herb lore, grounding, divination, bathing rites, candle magick, dreamwork, and so much more help you cultivate a spiritually fulfilling practice that won't empty your piggy bank. All the magickal components mentioned in this book are easy to find on the cheap at local grocery stores, discount stores, thrift stores, and online outlets. And you'll be amazed by how much you can do with what you already have. From the food in your fridge to the boxes full of abandoned projects, the potential for magick exists in every area of your life.

In the following pages, you'll find suggestions, rituals, and recipes for every budget. And when you understand the *why* behind the *what*, you can tailor them to what you have and where you are in your magickal journey. Got a garden full of herbs but no crystals? Swap in some clarifying lavender for quartz. Want to treat your witchcraft like a *Chopped* challenge, emptying your cabinets and closets and seeing which rituals you can perform? Rock out.

And on page 206, you'll find an intention key that makes it easy to choose alternatives in a pinch. A little creativity goes a long way when coupled with the magick that's already coursing through your veins.

This guide to truly *practical* magick was carefully created to work for every witch on the spectrum, from the magick-curious to the experienced practitioner. But, most of all, it's for all the witches who want to focus on the joy of witchcraft. Whether you're into cottagecore or kitchen witchery, science-based spellcraft or glamour magick, you'll find plenty within these pages that speaks to you. And you'll feel empowered to figure out what works for *you* as a witch, learning more about your own magick along the way.

If you're new to all this and a little unsure of where to start, then start at the beginning—aka "Witchcraft 101." It'll help you let go of the FOMO and carve out your own path forward. (Even if your baby-witch years are far behind you, it can help you hit the reset button.) Rituals, potions, spells, and recipes are scattered throughout the book, but don't feel pressured to dive in before you're ready. You'll find an index of all that good stuff at the back of the book so you can easily revisit it later. Getting back to basics means going at your own pace.

Will embracing authentic witchcraft magickally fix all of your problems and leave you with zero worries? Um, no. Nothing in this life does that (and you should be very afraid of anyone promising it). Will walking this path give you the opportunity to frolic in the moonlight, connect with your people, have powerful moments of self-reflection, play with potions and elixirs, find the magick in everyday life, and grow into the witch you were meant to be? Absolutely. So close those shopping tabs and dive in!

*You get to
decide which
kinds of magick
you practice.*

CHAPTER 1

Witchcraft 101

Substance Over Style

Whether you're a baby witch or a longtime practitioner, it's so easy to get caught up in the shopping aspect of magick. I know I did! All the gorgeous trappings, the polished aesthetic, and the ornate divination tools are part of what draws us to the practice—it's a whole new world beyond our regularly scheduled program of doing dishes and scrolling socials. And there's absolutely nothing wrong with enjoying those things. You just need a little (OK, a lot of) substance with that flash. That's what makes you a witch. But what that substance is for you will be different than what it is for your bestie. So let's do a deep dive and start figuring out what being a witch means to you. (Hint: Paring down on the extras and focusing on what feels natural helps.)

Who Can Be a Witch?

You. Them. Everyone. You can be a witch even if you've only read one magickal book in your whole life or tried two rituals ever. You can practice magick even if you only dabble a little in crystals or know the meaning of three Tarot cards. You can even tap into your power if you're a bit skeptical or other people tell you that you can't. You may be unsure of yourself or scared of your own power, but that's OK. You can be a witch. You are capable of magick. You have the Universe in your bones. You've got this.

But you probably need to learn a few things first, right? Right. Don't worry if you've jumped ahead and bought a whole slew of candles and crystals while wearing your best thrift-store velvets (#witchesofinstagram!). It's also cool if you saw a ritual on social media that you just *had* to try. You are the captain of your own ship, which means you get to approach witchcraft (and witchy books) choose-your-own-adventure style. (I know I have.) Just start wherever you are, and we'll work on embracing your inner witch together.

Your Personal Brand of Magick

While pop culture is really into witches right now, that definitely wasn't always the case. It's easy to get caught up with the social-media-driven aesthetic of the moment. "Aspirational" is one popular witch trend, which would be hilarious (given the history of witchcraft) if it wasn't so damaging in its own way. It's really just one more chance for people to tell us who we're supposed to be, how we're supposed to act and look, and what we're supposed to feel. Possibly more importantly, it's a way for them to tell us what we're supposed to buy—because we're *always* supposed to be buying something. But we don't need to buy into that BS.

What does it say about you if you don't look like, act like, speak like, and believe like the witches you see on social media or in pop culture? Are you really a witch? Yep! You are. I want you to know that I see you and I hold space for you as you are right now. Even if you're still figuring out what you want, even if you only dabble in magick occasionally, even if you don't feel like the word "witch" aligns with who you are, and even if you don't have an apartment full of aspirational witchy decor, I honor the magick inside you. There's enough room for all of us here at the table, and I will always save a seat for you.

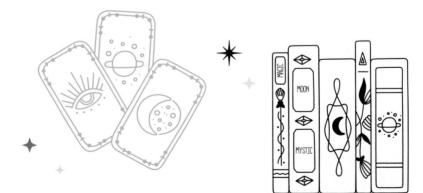

The Willing Student Self-Dedication Ritual

"Whoa, whoa, whoa! I haven't fully decided I even want to be a witch yet. How can I dedicate myself to something if I don't know that's what I want to do?" Good question! (And you *should* be asking questions like that, as we'll be discussing shortly.) First and foremost, all witchcraft should be based on consent. If you don't feel comfortable performing a ritual, practicing certain aspects of witchcraft, or communing with goddesses or spirits, you don't have to do it.

But the intention for this ritual isn't to dedicate yourself to witchcraft—it's to dedicate yourself to figuring out if becoming a witch and practicing witchcraft is the right path for you. That's it! Still, if you don't feel ready for a ritual yet, you can come back to this (or never come back to it). It's always your choice.

YOU'LL NEED:

- A tiny pinch of salt to center yourself in your intention

- Fresh rosemary sprigs to bring you knowledge, strength, and wisdom

- White cotton embroidery thread to symbolize the start of your journey

- A tealight to light the path for yourself

- A small bowl of water to connect you to your *genius loci*, or spirit of place (see page 100)

- A metal lid from a jar or a candle snuffer (optional)

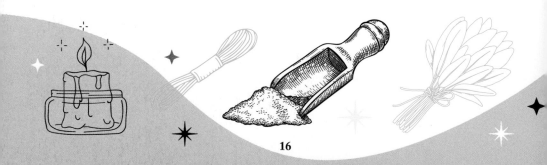

1. Take a few deep breaths. Concentrate on your intention and mindfully light the tealight. Put the pinch of salt under your tongue and let it dissolve.

2. Wrap the rosemary tightly from stem to tip with the embroidery thread, leaving enough thread at the stem for a loop. While holding your intention, carefully pass the rosemary bundle just over the top of the candle's flame three times. Then dip the rosemary into the water and gently tap yourself on the top of the head with it three times. (That's your crown chakra, which connects you to the Universe and the divine both inside and out.)

3. Cut another strand of embroidery thread that is long enough to fit around your ankle and tie it off with three knots. (You can also go all "friendship bracelet" on your anklet, but a single strand is fine.) Three is the number of wisdom, harmony, and understanding. This anklet will be a physical reminder of your intention.

4. Put the tealight somewhere firesafe and supervised for it to burn out, or use the jar lid or snuffer to extinguish the flame while you thank it for its presence in your ritual.

5. Last but not least, hang the rosemary bundle from its loop to dry. When your intention has manifested, you can leave the rosemary outside as an offering to the Universe.

Hot Tip

Alternatively, you can simmer the rosemary in a small pot of water, then waft the steam over your crown chakra and let the scent of rosemary fill your home. When you're finished, dispose of the rosemary *and* water outside as an offering.

Question Everything

You don't need to believe in all the things to be a witch. In fact, you should do the opposite. You should be looking at everything you learn—and everyone you learn it from—with a curious mind. Consider a person's motivation, their place in history, their privilege, their possible agenda, and anything else that might impact the information you're getting from them. Do this with goddesses, spirits, and ancestors that you work with; the witchy authors and influencers that you follow; the other witches in your life; and even yourself. Everyone (*everyone*) is subject to biases, preferences, and blind spots. (For one thing, the ancestors might not be up on the latest science and trends.) Be mindful about which practices and products really resonate with you, and which just sound good in the moment.

Mindful consumption is especially important these days, with spendy influencers hawking miracle cures, artisanal spells, and expensive crystals in every post. Are some things worth investing in? Sure. Are they necessary to your practice? Almost certainly not. You'll be amazed at how much magick is in the everyday objects and actions we take for granted. And, just like with any mindful practice, you'll discover what you really need as you go. Because the siren call of beautiful magickal objects is hard to resist, start by questioning the accounts you follow. Fill your feed with more accounts aligned with your values as a witch, and you'll be less tempted to buy things you don't need.

BROKE WITCH TIP

Challenge yourself to find rituals and spells you can do with what you have on hand before you invest in any new magickal ingredients or objects. (You'll find lots of them right here in this book to get you started!)

Trust Yourself

So, who can you trust? Yourself. Eventually. With practice. The truth is, in magick as in life, you will sometimes give yourself spectacularly bad advice. You're only human! But learning the difference between a whim and your actual intuition is a key part of your magickal evolution. Not only will it help you steer clear of potentially cocktail-infused, late-night purchases or sloppy, impulse-driven spellwork (not that I speak from experience or anything), it will also help you strengthen the magick that's already inside you. Because, when you trust your own intrinsic power, you can accomplish anything—with or without splashy extras or Instagrammable moments.

You can also use your intuition (combined with your habit of questioning everything) to figure out who else deserves your trust. You wouldn't take financial advice from someone with a spending problem, or love advice from someone whose longest relationship lasted three months, or pet-care advice from someone who kills succulents. So, maybe don't take witchcraft advice from a witch who throws lots of messy hexes and creates magickal chaos regularly. In other words, take any lessons with a grain of salt while looking at the *whole picture*. Even your ride-or-die bestie, who always knows the right thing to say and makes great choices for themselves, might not know what's best for you. Everyone is speaking from their own experience. You have to decide what works for you.

Tuning in to Your Intuition Ritual

One exercise or spell isn't going to give you an all-access pass to your intuition. It takes time and experience to start hearing your inner voice clearly. And, even then, you have to get good at separating it from your inner critic, social programming, and anxious thoughts. But that doesn't mean you can't help things along. The more you practice tapping into your intuition, the easier it'll get.

When you're all done, take a minute to write down any connections that jump out at you or any other feelings that crop up. You can come back to these later to see how things worked out. The more you do this, the easier it'll be to notice your intuition when it's tugging at your sleeve.

YOU'LL NEED:

↳ A notebook

↳ A pen or pencil

↳ A quiet space

DO THIS:

1. Sit in a comfortable, quiet spot. Visualize a column of white light coming down from above, filling you up, and then continuing deep into the ground below you. Once you feel connected to the magick, grab your notebook and pen.

2. Take three deep breaths and close your eyes, turning your attention inward to your body. What sensations do you notice? Scan your body and note any feelings that arise. Write down the first five things you notice.

3. Take another deep breath and close your eyes again, turning your attention inward to your mind. What sounds or words arise? What thoughts pop in? Write down the first five things you hear.

4. Take another deep breath and close your eyes again. What images arise in your mind's eye? A flash of a person, symbol, or scene? Write down the first five things you see.

Your Magickal Moral Compass

Figuring out what kind of witch you are or want to be starts with deciding what feels good to you—and what doesn't. Often, spiritual practices come with a list of rules. If you break any of those rules, there could be repercussions from peers or leaders in the spiritual community, from family, or even from the Divine. While there's nothing wrong with this approach to spirituality—it works for many people in many forms around the world—witchcraft doesn't work like that. As a witch, you need to determine for yourself what is and is not acceptable in your practice. Other witches may have a few suggestions for you based on their chosen practices, but, generally speaking, you need to develop your own moral code.

Can you do anything you want? Yes. Does that mean your actions are magickally, morally, or legally without consequences? No. Of course not. You could decide that arson is a mainstay of your practice, but that doesn't mean law enforcement is going to be on the same page. You don't get a special pass on being a good human just because you identify as a witch. (And, ideally, legality won't be the only thing guiding your moral compass as a witch.)

Wondering what all of this has to do with doing magick on the cheap? Figuring out your moral code as a witch helps you home in on the kind of craft you want to practice. And that can dictate which spirits you work with (and the kinds of offerings they require), what magickal ingredients and objects you need, how you source them, and more. We're still in the "figuring it out" phase here. Even if think you *have* figured it out, getting back to basics can give you a fresh perspective on what's really important to you and help you reel in any spendy habits that don't align with that.

A WITCH *by* ANY OTHER NAME

There isn't one right way to be a witch, but there are a lot of labels and specialties to choose from if any resonate with you. (And if none do, that's OK too!) Here are just a few:

- **Baby witches:** Beginner witches who are still finding their own path.

- **Cosmic witches:** The ones who know which planet is where at all times.

- **Folk witches:** Witches who practice magick passed down from person to person.

- **Green witches:** Plant-loving practitioners who draw their power from nature.

- **Gray witches:** Those who dance across the line between light and dark magick.

- **Hedge witches:** Practical witches who like to do their own thing and keep it simple.

- **House/Hearth witches:** Those who focus on making their homes feel magickal.

- **Kitchen witches:** Witches who incorporate magic into recipes and culinary rituals.

- **Sea witches:** Witches with a strong connection to the ocean.

Hot Take: Threefold Is a Comfortable Lie

When you practice witchcraft, you're causing lots of ripples in the Universe, and the Threefold Law is a common belief among witches addressing that. It essentially says that everything you do (good or bad) comes back to you threefold, and it usually comes with some pontification about karma. I'm assuming that the Threefold Law was something used to keep baby witches in line. But it's pretty flawed. The Law makes it sounds like if you are a good witch, a nice witch, then surely all of your spellwork will result in treats. So conversely, being a bad witch who has done some morally ambiguous deeds in your day would mean you deserve any terrible things that are happening to you. That's . . . a lot to unpack. But let's try.

"Deserve" is a fraught concept to begin with. Do you think everyone who has a posh career, a perfect family, great sex, and everything they could ever possibly want *deserves* it? Probably not, no. And nothing is as perfect as it appears from the outside, so you might be glossing over a long list of big and small heartbreaks and injustices that they also did not deserve. That person may not even enjoy their life, no matter how much you would like to enjoy it for them.

This is also not really how karma actually works in the incredibly old spiritual tradition in which it's grounded. Karma is messy, it's complicated, and it takes lifetimes to unravel. Someone who appears to have an easy life could be burning off karma they've acquired over lifetimes (or just be really good at curating their social media profiles). Someone who appears to have a very difficult life could be dealing with the fallout of some *really* bad stuff three lives ago. You could have saved the right spider, annoyed the wrong spirit, or been blessed by an ancestor who really likes the cut of your jib. The point is, who knows? Is it worth spending a lot of time and energy on trying to unravel life's mysteries? Or is it better instead to live your life in such a way that, most of the time, you sleep soundly? Yeah, the last one. And that means living in tune with your own moral compass.

Calibrating Your Compass

Hey, you know what's free? Figuring out which way is north on your magickal moral compass. Once you do, you can tailor your practice to it. Knowing your core values helps you decide where you want to spend your time, energy, *and* money. Keep in mind that the answers to some of these questions may change for you with time and practice. That's OK! Make it a habit to check in with yourself every so often, and your practice will always reflect the kind of witch you want to be. Here are a few journaling prompts to get you started (don't overthink your responses—let your gut take the lead):

- Is it ever acceptable to use magick on someone else (e.g., for healing)? Why or why not?

- Why do you think most love spells are discouraged in witchcraft?

- How do you feel about using magick to cut ties with someone in your life? Why?

- Is it OK to use magick to bring yourself material wealth? Why or why not?

- How do you want to source your magickal components?

- If buying components from a store, does it matter how the store or manufacturer treats their employees?

- When working magick with a group or coven, do you need to agree with everyone present?

- If someone hurts you—intentionally or unintentionally—is it OK to use magick to hurt them back? Why or why not?

You Are the Compass Rose

Many magickal practices use directions in ritual work as a way to orient the practitioner in both this world and the unseen world. And as long as we're talking moral compasses, it seems like a good time to discuss how your core values relate to those directions. Who you are as a witch and what you value affect how your magick manifests.

Generally speaking, each direction is associated with certain elements and aspects. We will start with the East, where the sun rises. The East is associated with the element of air, which covers aspects of your spirit like your intellect and inspiration. South is associated with fire and things like passion and transformation. West is associated with water, emotions, and intuition. North is associated with earth as well as with your body and balance. The center is the Universe itself, whose energy radiates outward. How you connect to that energy impacts its use in your magick. In other words, you are the compass rose in your practice.

YOU'LL NEED:

- A compact mirror
- A notebook (aka grimoire)
- A pen or pencil
- A compass (or compass app)

1. Pick a place in your home where you can be alone. Using your compass, face east. Close your eyes and take a few centering breaths. Think about your core values relating to your intellect and creativity. Write them down.

2. Next, face south. Close your eyes, take another centering breath, and think about your core values relating to passion and your own personal evolution. Write them down.

3. Next, face west. With closed eyes, take a centering breath and think about your core values relating to your mental health, emotional wellness, and intuition. Write them down.

4. Lastly, face north. Close your eyes, take a centering breath, and think about your core values relating to your body and internal equilibrium. Write them down.

5. Now look in the mirror and look at yourself, your own compass rose. Consider your core values, your own divine nature, and your connection to the Universe. Write down your guiding principles. Place your hands on the paper and say (out loud or in your mind): *And so it is.*

Hot Tip

Figuring out your values is a great place to start, but things change. Write the date on these pages and come back to them every so often. Think about what's changed, if anything, and why. You can journal about it or even do the exercise all over again.

Your Will and Your Wants

As my occult aunties say, you have to know what you want to get it. That's even more true with witchcraft, which requires clear intentions to practice it. And it's not just for the spellwork—creating the practice itself also requires intention and clarity. One of the more exciting aspects of witchcraft is that every witch's practice is bespoke, meaning it's made just for you (by you). You get to decide which kinds of magick you practice, what kinds of components feel right to you, and who else is going to be involved. But, like everything good in life, creating a magickal practice takes work. That's where your willpower comes in. You have to commit to doing the work.

Designing Your Practice

Once you know what you truly value, you can start designing a practice that reflects it. What do you want yours to look like? Do you like the aesthetic aspect of arranging your altar just so or the practical applications of magickal objects? Did you turn to magick to achieve your goals or live everyday life with intention? Do you want to learn more about yourself and work to heal some past wounds? Are you soothed by the ritual of rituals or fascinated by the scientific connection with the Universe? Do you want to connect with goddesses, spirits, and ancestors, or bond over coffee and casting with your fellow witches?

There are so many possibilities within the world of witchcraft and absolutely no wrong answers. Your practice could include a combination of any of these aspects, or of all of these aspects and more. It could depend on the day, your mood, or what you have in your pantry. But whatever it looks like, it should help you feel empowered in your life because it's adding something to it, whether a deeper connection to yourself, a sense of belonging, moments of joy, or even feeling seen as a witch through likes on socials (no judgment here!).

WHAT *is* INTENTION, ANYWAY?

An intention is essentially a goal with feeling behind it, and it's a key component of magick. You can't do anything without first getting clear on your intention. When it comes to spellwork with multiple components, setting an intention is basically telling each item what it's there for, because every crystal and herb has multiple uses (which is why, by the way, you don't need to buy every magickal object in the store—but more on that in Chapter 2). It's also a way to communicate what you want to the Universe. That's why, in folklore, saying names and words out loud is important; there's always someone or something listening. For more on intention, see page 78.

Follow Your Heart and Your Brain

What is your true heart's desire? As the protagonist in your fairytale, this question is at the root of your witchcraft. For some, it will be an easy one to answer. For others, it's more complicated. Maybe you've hit some discouraging roadblocks along the way that have you constantly waiting for the other shoe to drop. We can be so afraid to fail or so afraid of the failures we've encountered in our process that we talk ourselves out of what we really want for ourselves. But, with magick, anything is possible. (Mostly.)

The trick to making your dreams come true is making sure those dreams are yours. Maybe you tend to put the needs of others before your own, or you worry about what others will think. Or maybe you're really just trying to keep up with the Joneses because you're envious of what they have. (When you're watching someone else's fairytale, it's easy to montage past the difficult parts and zoom in on how good they seem to have it now.) But for witchcraft to work well, it has to come from the heart. All the expensive crystals and pendulums and candles are worthless without clear intention behind them. And you'd be amazed at how much money you can save when you're not trying to appease other people.

Maybe you worry that your true desires are frivolous. World peace? Totally acceptable to want. A great career and beautiful home? Check and check. But saying you want to be knee-deep in adventure when you're seventy, or you want to have over 100,000 followers on Instagram and wake up every morning to a mountain of boxes full of complimentary designer goods? That's going to raise some eyebrows from other people. But who cares? You and your heart's desires are not beholden to other people; they are beholden to *you*. And magick doesn't judge. So, what do you really want?

Witchcraft gives you an opportunity to dream as big as you can. Will your dreams all come true? Probably not. Life happens, and not even magick or money can fix everything. Will some of your dreams come true? Yes. Definitely. It's worth a try, right?

DON'T LET FEAR STOP YOU

One word of caution: fear of getting what you want is a very real thing. We've all heard the old adage "be careful what you wish for because you might just get it." It's usually used as a way to keep small children in line when they wish their parents away (à la Kevin McCallister in *Home Alone*). But if you're afraid to get what you want, that fear is going to infuse and impede your magick. Luckily, it's usually not hard to figure out what you would struggle with receiving.

Considering scale and scope is important, even when dreaming as big as you can. It will keep you focused on your desire because you'll actually want the outcome you get. Maybe becoming a rock star and playing to sold-out stadiums doesn't jibe with your social anxiety, but performing solo to thousands on social media feels great. And if you're not happy with the result? That's OK! It happens all the time, and it's one of the best ways to refine your intention so you can get it right next time. Now that you're a little wiser, you can start working toward a new and better-aligned dream. Just get clear on what you *really* want, and the rest will work itself out.

Asking for What You Want

Once you know what you want, all that's left is to ask for it. For many, that's harder than it sounds. But if you don't ask for what you want—whether it's from a romantic partner, a parent, a bestie, or a boss—you won't often get it. Sometimes that's because others don't know you want it, and sometimes it's because others don't know how important it is to you. It's the same with magick; you need to communicate what you want and how much you want it. In witchcraft, you might ask the Universe, goddesses, spirits, ancestors, or even yourself for what you want. And to communicate it clearly, you need to combine intention with action (aka spellwork). If you're feeling a little unsure, start small with what you have and work your way up to the bigger stuff. This incremental approach will not only help you get clear on what you want, it will also help you gauge what's worth investing in and what's not.

Your Will Is Your Witchcraft

Once you know what you want, and you've set your intention, you're just a quick Bibbidi-bobbidi-boo away from living your best life, right? Not quite. Now you have to put in the work. Real magick isn't like it is on TV, where the main character snaps her fingers or wiggles her nose and instantly manifests her every desire. It takes time, patience, and plenty of physical effort. And, like life itself, your practice will be filled with pitfalls and pauses that can keep you from accomplishing your goals—if you let them. It's up to you to follow through even when you absolutely do not want to.

Your will is a deliberate, fixed manifestation of your desire and intention. Let's unpack that. Say you want to run a marathon. That's not something you can leap out of bed one day and do. (I mean, you can. But you probably won't get very far into said marathon.) You'd have to train for it over a long period of time, right? Suddenly your joints are feeling crunchy, and you're faced with having to sacrifice your lazy Sunday-morning brunches with friends. But if you want to run that marathon—or achieve that big magickal dream of yours—you need to tap into your will to get you through the hard parts so that you keep making progress. It'll be worth it! Plus, your will *strengthens* your intention, making your magick even more powerful.

Ground and Center

One thing that can help with your will, your wants, *and* your magick is a grounding ritual. Taking a moment to ground and center yourself refocuses your will on what is actually important to you. This is a pivotal ritual that you need to get really comfy-cozy with as a witch. You can do it whenever you're feeling overwhelmed, disconnected, or impulsive—like when you're ready to hit "buy now" on a cart full of crystal-infused candles.

This ritual gives you a chance to call your energy back to yourself if it's wandered away from you in the moment. Using a simple visualization, you'll reconnect to the earth to stabilize your spirit and use the energy of the stars in the sky to recharge it and burn away any negativity you want to release. Bonus: This comes with zero cost and requires zero components, and you can do it anytime, anywhere. But it's best if you can sit upright with your back supported and feet flat on the floor.

DO THIS:

1. Start by taking a few deep breaths. If you want to, you can close your eyes for the exercise. Take a moment to let go of the stresses and excitement of the day and focus on being present with yourself and your breath.

2. Now, imagine yourself as a tree. How the tree looks is up to you. It can be an ordinary weeping willow or have bark made out of gumdrops and leaves made out of cotton candy—whatever works best for you. Once you're embodying the tree, imagine roots growing out of the bottoms of your feet, through the floor, and into the deep, loamy earth.

3. Take another deep breath in and draw soothing, grounding energy up from your roots and into your body. Exhale any negative vibes. Repeat this two more times.

4. Next, imagine yourself growing branches from the top of your head that spiral up into the stars in the sky. Inhale deeply, then draw the stars' energy down through your body and roots and into the earth. Exhale anything that's not serving you.

5. Inhale and draw energy up through your roots, through your body, out past the branches, and into the sky. Exhale anything you don't need in this moment. Repeat this six more times.

6. When you are finished, open your eyes (if they're closed) and say to the Universe: *And so it is.*

All you need is a little know-how and your own intrinsic power.

CHAPTER 2

The Broke Witch Basics

Embrace Witchy Minimalism

If you're attracted to magick for the trappings, you're not alone. Glittering crystals, small leather-bound books, stacks of Tarot cards printed on rich paper, obscure herbs with entrancing scents, a rainbow of candles, handmade altar tools—it's all just so intoxicating. And that's before we even get to the clothes! Who wouldn't love an excuse to fill their home with shiny new things imbued with potentially life-changing properties?

And it's not just the sense of newness and possibility that gets you. Now that there's so much positive representation in the media about witches and witchcraft, it's easy to get stuck on what a witch should be and have. (I'm twenty years in, and I still do some days.) But before you buy all the things and act out your own witchy makeover montage, take a deep breath. For one thing, if you're reading this book, you probably don't have a trust fund to bankroll a magickal spending spree. For another, you don't need to.

I'm going to be your cliché fairy godmother and bestow you with a bit of wisdom: You don't need to change a thing to be a "real witch." Your witchcraft has been inside you all along. (Things are cliché for a reason, Grasshopper.) Witchcraft is about both the practical work and the magickal work. It's about your will and your desire. You can create beauty and feel empowered with very little in the way of newly purchased shiny objects.

Does that mean you need literally nothing to be a witch? Some witches would argue that is indeed the case. Your will alone may be enough to manifest your intention through your witchcraft and practice. That said, it's a bit tougher for a new witch. And, just between us, it's probably a bit less fun too. But you don't need to break the bank to make magick happen, so let's keep it simple! (At least for now.) All you need is a little know-how and your own intrinsic power.

You'll be amazed by how much you can do when you start with the right herbs, crystals, oils, and tools. By choosing magickal multitaskers, you can minimize the expense while still maximizing your magick. That's because your biggest investment will be energetic—your intention does the heavy lifting. All the pretty things and enticing scents are extras. And when you're not caught up in the aesthetics, you can get back to that authentic connection that makes your magick so awesome.

Magick-Making Flora

Salts, herbs, spices, and flowers are all commonly used in magick. Why? Because they've been around since the beginning of time and contain all the natural magick of the Universe. Each one offers its own special blend of magickal properties, used for centuries in not only mysticism but also medicinal practices. The colors, scents, and flavors of plants combine with the way they exist in the world to contribute power and beauty to all sorts of spells. And as a special bonus for broke witches, finding them is as easy as foraging in your backyard or strolling through your local grocery store.

In the following pages you'll find twenty of the most commonly used plants, herbs, and spices to add to your witchy toolkit. Twenty might seem like a lot, but even the most reluctant cooks will have at least a few of these in their cabinets already. Most are regular grocery-store staples and everyday kitchen ingredients that you'll want to keep around. (If there's one thing you're going to learn from this book, it's that there's magick in ordinary things.) And if you've got the patience and even a tiny bit of sunlit space, you can skip the middleman and grow your own (see page 101). This also means you can make sure your flowers and herbs are culinary grade, so you will be able to use them in teas, tonics, and more.

But you certainly don't need all of these right this minute. Give yourself time to enjoy the process of stocking your witchy pantry. There's no medal in magick for buying everything at once. Instead, read through the plant profiles and think about your goals and priorities. Focus on the ingredients that will help you meet them. (You'll notice more than a little overlap in magickal properties, so you have your pick.) This is a great opportunity to explore your local shops and see who has what in the way of spices—among other things. You never know what other inexpensive magickal components you may find in your adventures.

Allspice

Allspice, with its warm and spicy aroma, is associated with luck, prosperity, healing, and protection. It can help you attract money, ward off evil, and enhance your psychic abilities. You'll want to  stock this versatile spice in whole form, which you can find easily at grocery stores and online. (Organic and fair-trade options are always worth the splurge if you can swing it.) But you can also use ground allspice if that's what you have on hand. You can add this spice to prosperity candles, protective charms, or divination rituals.

Basil

Super cheap, easy to find or grow, and infinitely useful, basil is a must-have for all witches. With a fresh and minty aroma, basil is associated with wealth, success, and protection. It can boost your confidence, attract prosperity, and create a peaceful environment. You can find this fragrant herb in fresh or dried form at farmers' markets and grocery stores, or you can grow it in a pot on your kitchen windowsill. Add it to foods to diffuse tension, bring it to work in a charm bag to ensure success, and stir it into salves for luck.

Bay Leaves

Bay leaves can do a lot more than spice a soup. Their magickal associations include wisdom, success, happiness, and manifestation. They can enhance your intuition, protect you from negativity, and help you achieve your goals. You'll find this herb in dried form at most grocery stores and online if you don't happen to have a bay laurel tree nearby. You can write your wishes on bay leaves and burn them, put them under your pillow for prophetic dreams, make a protection sachet with them, or use them to bless spaces.

CEDAR CHIPS

Cedar chips aren't an herb or a flower, but they deserve an honorable mention in this section for imbuing your spells with confidence, strength, power, and a delightfully earthy, insect-repelling scent. Cedar is also associated with healing, harmony, prosperity, protection, and purification. That's a lot of magickal bang for your buck! You can find cedar chips online, cedar shavings in the pet section of the big box stores, or cedar mulch at your local garden store—they all get the job done.

Cardamom

Another easy-to-find pantry staple, cardamom can help with communication, creativity, mental clarity, and learning. It can also attract love, luck, and prosperity, as well as ward off negative energies and evil spirits. Sprinkle cardamom in your wallet to attract abundance, burn cardamom incense to inspire clarity, or add some spice (literally *and* metaphorically) to a romantic dinner.

Chamomile

Linked with peace, healing, sleep, and stress relief, chamomile is one of the most gentle and versatile magickal herbs. You can grow your own at home with even a mildly green thumb, but you don't need fresh flowers for spellwork (although the petals make a lovely addition to bath rituals). Dried chamomile works fine, and it's easy to find—just snip open inexpensive chamomile tea bags and empty their contents into a cute upcycled jar! Add this soothing herb to healing salves, sleep sachets, and teas to bring out its best.

Cinnamon

Associated with the energy of success, money, and luck, cinnamon is one of the great magickal multitaskers. And, lucky for you, it's cheap and easy to find at any grocery store. Even some dollar stores carry it. There's no need to spring for cinnamon sticks, although they can be a delightful addition to simmer pots (see page 122). Ground cinnamon will usually do the trick. You can blow this cozy spice over your doorstep on the first of the month to attract abundance, add a pinch to any brew to amp up its energy, and make it the star of money spells.

SWEPT UP *in* CINNAMON

Inexpensive cinnamon brooms start popping up in stores around Halloween, but these aren't just cheesy decorations. Hanging one by your door can protect your home and attract abundance. Plus, you can use it to sweep out bad vibes and cleanse your space before spellwork.

Honey is basically liquid magick. Those cheap, bear-shaped bottles will do the job, but honey is one ingredient that's splurge-worthy. Organic local honey can infuse your magick with a little extra oomph thanks to its close connection with your natural world. You can even find honey that has been infused with other things, like lavender (great for sleep) or citrus (for positivity). Use honey in spells to sweeten someone toward you (friend or love— it's all-purpose), leave it as an offering, put it in a healing salve, or even keep a jar of it on your altar to help spells manifest.

Cloves

Cloves are just as strong and distinctive in their magickal uses as they are in their culinary ones. They can help with protection, banishing, courage, and justice (even putting a stop to annoying gossip). They can also help you attract love, money, and success, as well as cleanse and purify spaces and objects. Not bad for such a little bud that you can find on any grocery store's shelves. You can use a few—or seven, for extra luck—in protective spell jars or cleansing bath rituals, stir them (ground) into baked goods, or burn them like incense.

Ginger

Ginger is a powerful plant with a rich, spicy flavor and a long history as a healing herb. Its magickal associations include love, success, protection, luck, prosperity, and energy. Ginger can also add a little spice and adventure to your life, both in the bedroom and out in the world. Add it to spells and recipes to speed things up, ignite passion, or just boost their positive intentions. (It's also really great in tea when you're under the weather—both magickally and medicinally.)

Lavender

Lavender, with its soothing and calming aroma, is a magickal powerhouse associated with peace, happiness, and relaxation. It can help you attract love, promote healing, and bring peace and tranquility to pretty much any situation (even those run-ins with your ex). You'll want to stock this gentle herb in dried form, which you can find cheaply online and at craft stores. (Don't sleep on those coupons!) Even tea bags will work in a pinch. You can add lavender to a healing bath, a centering oil, a restful sachet under your pillow, and so much more. But for any edible recipes, make sure you use culinary-grade or homegrown lavender to avoid ingesting any harmful chemicals.

Lemon

One of the most useful additions to any magickal pantry (or, in this case, the fridge) is the lemon. Not only is it inexpensive to come by, you can also use just about every part of it—the fruit, the juice, and the peel—in spellwork. This bright and refreshing fruit is associated with happiness, cleansing, and purification. Place a couple slices in a bowl of salt to dispel negative energy, add the peels to rituals to break ties with the past, or stir some juice into a day-brightening tea (see page 129).

Mint

Mint's multitasking prowess goes beyond witchcraft—it's scientifically proven to improve focus, numb pain, and improve digestion. Add to that its magickal associations with communication, clarity, prosperity, and vitality, and you can see why mint is worth having on hand. Bonus: Mint basically grows itself (which is why you should keep it in its own container—this plant can't keep its roots to itself). You can use it in refreshing recipes and teas, clarifying simmer pots, and vibe-raising spells.

Nutmeg

Who doesn't have a little jar of nutmeg left over from Thanksgivings past? You may as well put it to good use. (Not that pumpkin pie isn't a perfectly good use!) This sweet, warm spice is especially useful for attracting luck, enhancing psychic abilities, breaking hexes, and promoting good dreams. You can sprinkle some into a sachet for under your pillow to induce prophetic dreams or add a dash to your tea to boost your intuition. You can also carry a whole nutmeg in your pocket or purse to increase your luck, confidence, and prosperity.

DON'T FORGET the TREES!

Cedar isn't the only tree with magickal oomph. And whether you live in a cottage in the woods (every green witch's dream) or in a big city, you can find a twig or two to incorporate into your practice.

- **Birch:** Cleansing, purification, and protection.
- **Maple:** Love, prosperity, and abundance.
- **Oak:** Strength, courage, protection, luck, and fertility.
- **Pine:** Cleansing, clarity, prosperity, and protection.
- **Willow:** Love, growth, renewal, harmony, and healing.

Red Pepper

Another pantry staple you can pick up at the dollar store, red pepper flakes add heat and energy to your magickal workings. They're especially handy for protection, banishing, justice, and courage. Sprinkle some around a space to cleanse it or use them in spells to move people out of your life or speed things up. You can also use this fiery spice to promote fidelity or to boost your confidence and fortitude in challenging situations.

Rose Petals

With their enchanting beauty and scent, roses are a versatile magickal ingredient in all things relating to love, beauty, romance, glamour, and healing. You can add dried rose petals to teas, charm bags, and bath rituals to deepen relationships, or use them in your self-care practices to promote emotional well-being, relieve stress, and foster inner harmony. They can also make a pretty and edible topping for desserts.

BROKE WITCH TIP

Roses are expensive. But guess what? Magick doesn't care if you get your rose petals from half-price roses at the grocery store after Valentine's Day. Whenever you see some on sale, hang them to dry and save the petals for future (non-edible) spells. (You'll need culinary-grade petals for use in teas or baked goods.)

Rosemary

Said to flourish around powerful feminine energy, rosemary represents creativity, healing, and wisdom. This common herb isn't just readily available on the cheap at any grocery store, it's also super easy to grow in your witch's garden, even if that garden is a plastic cup on your kitchen windowsill. Dried rosemary can give you a lot of magickal bang for your buck, but some spells call for the fresh stuff. It can be added to healing teas, protective potions, and cleansing spells. (It's also great with charcuterie— see page 120.)

Sage

Sage has a long history of use in spiritual and magickal practices, particularly for its ability to cleanse negative energy and provide protection. Common sage's cousin, white sage, is often burned as a sacred herb in smudging ceremonies. (But it's not the only herb that can cleanse a space— rosemary works well, too.) You can use common sage as a culinary herb in recipes and teas to boost creativity and soothe anxiety.

Salt

Salt, with its protective and purifying properties, is a magickal essential that can ward off negative energies and cleanse your space and tools. One peek at the food aisle in HomeGoods will tell you that there's an endless variety out there, and each has its own magickal specialty (more on that on page 113). All you really need, though, is regular old table salt. Use it to create a protective circle around you—yes, just like in *Hocus Pocus*—create a cleansing spray for your home, or top off a banishing jar.

Star Anise

In addition to making a tasty mulled wine or cider, star anise can bring you luck, power, and protection—not to mention enhancing your magickal abilities and intuition. You'll want to skip the regular grocery stores, which put a premium on whole spices, and buy this one at your local Asian market or online. Then you can add it to divination teas, prosperity charms, manifestation rituals, sleep sachets, and so much more. You can even place a pod above your doors and windows for a little added peace of mind.

PROTECTION BLEND

Getting clear on your intention not only can make your magick stronger but also can save you money. Case in point: Italian seasoning typically includes thyme, basil, oregano, rosemary—all protective herbs. So if protection is your main goal, you can hold off on buying each herb separately and just buy an inexpensive blend.

Thyme

A powerful herb with a fresh and inviting scent, thyme is associated with courage, strength, and confidence as well as affection and loyalty. It can help you achieve your goals, stand up for yourself, and overcome your fears. And if you use your oven for more than storing sweaters, it's probably already in your cupboard. (It's also an easy addition to your witch's garden.) Use fresh or dried thyme in a success sachet, a power oil, or a protection wash.

Violets

Consider this your excuse to go foraging in springtime! Sweet violets are readily available for free in most of North America and have a variety of magickal uses. This wildflower is associated with love, harmony, peace, protection, sleep, and intuition and can help you attract romance, ward off evil, and even enhance your psychic abilities. You can gather a bunch when they're at their peak (and taking over yards everywhere) and dry them for later use in protective charms, sleep sachets, and more. If you know your patch of violets is pesticide free (or you find culinary-grade edible violets on sale), you can even add them to tinctures and teas.

Glam It Up Ritual

Want to experiment with glamour magick and give yourself a boost of *je ne sais quoi* in your daily life? (The French are renowned for their beguiling charm, so why not the rest of us?) This little spell jar is just the thing. It can help you feel your most alluring, attract and enhance positivity, and protect your energy. Keep it close to you—as a necklace, on your headboard, or in your purse—to get the maximum effect.

YOU'LL NEED:

- A pink candle, anointed with rose water to increase your glamour (optional)
- A candle holder (optional)
- Rose petals to attract others
- Dried violets to uplift your vibes
- Pink Himalayan salt to banish negative vibes from others
- A tiny corked jar
- Red sealing wax

DO THIS:

1. Focus on your glamourous intention (e.g., to feel your most bewitching). If using a candle, place it in its holder and light it with this intention in mind.

2. Layer your flowers and salt in the jar to fill it. Breathe your intention into the jar.

3. Seal the jar with the cork, then pass it carefully over the pink candle (if using a candle).

4. Finish sealing the jar with the sealing wax to keep it shut tight.

Just the Crystals You Need

You might not come across cinnamon or rosemary in the wild, but crystals are pretty much everywhere. They're just hard to spot because they look like, well, rocks. It's a lot easier (and incredibly tempting) to buy them already picked and polished at your local craft store or favorite metaphysical shop. That's why lot of new witches start with crystal magick. Plus, you can arrange, display, and admire crystals purely for their beauty, and using them can feel a little more exciting than rooting around a spice cabinet for bay leaves. But crystals are like potato chips—it's hard to stop at just one. And that adds up fast.

The good news is, you can do a lot with just a few crystals. Plus, each crystal has different vibes to it. You may connect more strongly with some rather than others, just like you like certain tastes and smells more than others. Curating your collection little by little will deepen your spiritual connection to your crystals, save you money, streamline your spellwork, and leave you room to grow your practice.

You can keep a crystal close to you to amp up vibes for certain intentions or to ground yourself in stressful situations. You can even use crystals to keep away unwanted attention at events or from specific people by keeping the right crystal close. Keeping a tiny chip of a certain crystal in your wallet can help keep your wallet full. You can keep a chip of crystal over a specific chakra to bring healing energy to that chakra. The following crystals are easy to find and will do a lot of the heavy lifting in your collection of witchy components.

Amethyst

Amethyst, with its stunning purple hue, is associated with healing, clarity, calm, spirituality, wisdom, and protection. It can help you connect with your higher self, enhance your psychic powers, and shield you from negative energies.

Aquamarine

Soothing blue-green aquamarine is associated with insight, truth, wisdom, healing, and courage. It can help you calm emotions, heal wounds, and overcome fears.

Citrine

Considering its bright yellow-orange color, it's no wonder that citrine is associated with fire, wealth, success, and joy. It can help you attract abundance, boost your confidence, and energize your spirit. You can use citrine for manifestation, creativity, optimism, and so much more.

BROKE WITCH TIP

While larger crystals are lovely, and you may eventually vibe with certain stones that you will want to have in larger sizes, the crystal chips you can get at a craft store for jewelry making are perfect for new witches. They're inexpensive enough that it's no big deal if you lose some, so you can use them in your witchcraft with wild abandon while you are still figuring out which components really speak to you.

Clear Quartz

If you can only afford to buy one magickal object, make it clear quartz. This inexpensive crystal is associated with light, clarity, cleansing, healing, and power but can be subbed in for any crystal in any spell, conforming to your intention. Plus, it can amplify your witchcraft.

Green Aventurine

Sparkling with gold flecks, green aventurine is associated with luck, prosperity, growth, harmony, and confidence. It can help you attract opportunities and abundance as well as enhance your well-being. Green aventurine is especially handy in spells for luck, money, and healing.

Hematite

Hematite can be used in spells relating to grounding, balancing, protection, strength, and courage. This metallic-silver crystal can help you dispel negative energy, shield yourself from harm, and boost your confidence and willpower. Because of its iron content, this is one crystal you shouldn't leave in water.

Lava Stone

Lava stone, with its porous black or brown color and volcanic origin, is associated with fire, transformation, and creativity but also stability and endurance. It can help you release anger, overcome challenges, and stay grounded and calm. Plus, it can absorb essential oils and enhance their aromatherapy benefits.

Moonstone

Moonstone's milky iridescence lends itself to intuition, dreams, emotions, and femininity. It can help you enhance your psychic abilities, access your subconscious, and honor your cycles and feelings. Moonstone is also great for growth, stability, and new beginnings.

Rose Quartz

Soft pink rose quartz has a gentle, positive energy associated with love, compassion, forgiveness, and healing. It can help you attract love, heal your heart, and cultivate self-love and acceptance.

Selenite

Milky selenite, which is known as the goddess stone, is associated with purification, protection, harmony, and healing. It can ward against negative energy when placed above doorways or cleanse and charge other crystals and components.

Smoky Quartz

Like the other quartz crystals, smoky quartz is great for grounding, cleansing, and balancing your energy. It can help you clear negative thoughts, emotions, and energies as well as protect you from psychic attacks, stress, and environmental pollution. Plus, it can give you a creative boost.

Tiger's Eye

Tiger's eye is a golden-brown, banded crystal that can help you boost your courage, confidence, and creativity. It also has protective properties and can help you ground yourself and overcome fear, anxiety, and self-doubt.

CLEANSING and CHARGING CRYSTALS

Your crystals need to be recharged just like you do. But while you need food, sleep, and water to recharge, your crystals likely find the occasional full-moon-lit "soak" in a bowl of salt to be enough. Alternatively, you could run them under water or sit them on a sunny windowsill. Just do a quick Google search to make sure your particular crystal is water and salt safe first.

THE SPIRIT *in the* STONE

In animism, which many witches practice, it's believed that *all* objects have a spirit, from grass and herbs to dirt and crystals to copy machines (at least Marie Kondo and I believe that last one). Does that mean everything has a consciousness? Not necessarily. Certainly not in ways that most of us would understand. But objects—like crystals—resonate with certain vibrations. For example, rose-quartz crystals tend to resonate with love in all its forms. And the more you work with a crystal, the more it opens communication between yourself and the crystal. In other words, you develop a relationship with your crystals. Does that mean that a rock is going to start talking to you? Probably not. But it's possible that your rose quartz could sense your intention when you do love-related witchcraft and want to lend its energy to it.

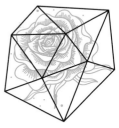

Making Friends with Clear Quartz

As we've discussed, clear quartz is the go-to crystal for just about every intention because it's a natural amplifier. What would you like to amplify in your life? Do you want more sizzle in the bedroom? More money in your wallet? More success in your studies or career? Pick a fairly simple intention in just one area in your life (you don't want to overwhelm your new friend), then follow this ritual to amplify it. It's that easy!

YOU'LL NEED:

- A clear quartz crystal
- Your journal or grimoire

DO THIS:

1. Hold your crystal and take some centering breaths.

2. Tell your crystal out loud what you want it to amply in your life over the next week. Let it know that you'll be keeping it close—on your desk, in your car, or wherever feels right.

3. Every night, before you go to bed, write down any amplification you have noticed in your intended area. Then thank your crystal for its help, even if it was just in some small way.

Essential Essential Oils

No magickal practice would be complete without essential oils, right? Not necessarily. As you're hopefully learning, you can do a lot with a little. What really matters is your intention—all the herbs, crystals, and oils are just sprinkles on your sundae. (But they are really delicious, sweet-smelling sprinkles!) Essential oils align your sense of smell with your intention. You can make your own magickal blends to wear, add them to a diffuser for sleeping, or use them to enhance your ritual work.

You can also use oils to anoint magickal objects (like candles) or yourself. *Anointing* means to make something extra sacred or to align your object with your intention. If you anoint a candle by dabbing three drops of lavender oil on it while holding the intention for your roommates to stop arguing in the living room so you can watch Netflix in peace, you are aligning that candle to do a specific sacred task for you. (After all, binge-watching *is* sacred.) While you can use dried herbs for this, the oiling of objects is something that humans have been performing in various spiritual practices basically since we figured out that we could do it. Oils are used to make something holy, whereas dried herbs are able to multitask because we can eat them, burn them, and use them in daily life.

So, essential oils can be an incredibly powerful addition to your practice. Just remember that this isn't a sprint. You don't have to buy all the oils immediately or fill your witchy pantry with oils for every possible occasion. For the most powerful magick, you want to save your money, start small, and curate your collection mindfully. (And check out discount department stores for inexpensive sets, which are plentiful now that oil diffusers are popular.) The essential oils that follow are all affordable and easy to obtain. And, magickally, they cover all the bases!

Cedar

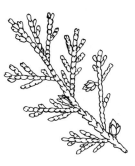

Cedar essential oil can help you connect with the earth element and your ancestors. It can also cleanse negative energy, protect you from harm, and attract abundance, luck, success, and prosperity. Plus, it has that amazingly warm, woodsy aroma.

Frankincense

Frankincense essential oil is a sacred oil that's been used for thousands of years in spiritual practices. It has a spicy, uplifting scent and can help promote intuition, vitality, healing, peace, and purification. It can also be useful in banishing spells.

Lavender

Like the herb itself, lavender essential oil is as versatile as it is soothing. It's associated with love, creativity, harmony, healing, relaxation, and happiness. You can also use it to consecrate tools and spaces for your spellwork.

Lemon

Lemon essential oil is a bright, energizing magickal component that can help you clear your mind, focus your intention, and manifest your goals. You can also use it to purify spaces, repel negativity, boost confidence, and enhance love in all its forms.

Just because essential oils are made from herbs and flowers doesn't mean you can use them the same way. You might add culinary-grade lavender buds to your tea, but you should never ingest essential oils. This is highly concentrated stuff. Even when you use them on your skin, you always want to dilute them with a carrier oil and do a patch test. And make sure you keep essential oils away from pets. Are there some exceptions to these rules? Sure. But better safe than sorry.

Jasmine

Jasmine essential oil has a sweet, floral scent that can uplift your mood and attract love even before you incorporate this oil into your spellwork. Magickally, it can enhance your intuition and psychic abilities as well as help you connect with the divine feminine. You can also use jasmine in spells for attraction, passion, and love (romantic and otherwise).

Orange

Bright and cheerful orange essential oil can boost your energy and creativity, attract abundance, and ensure success, which makes it a great addition to a variety of spells. It can also help you overcome fear and anxiety as well as cultivate joy and optimism.

Patchouli

Patchouli essential oil is a powerful and earthy oil that can ground you and protect you from negative energies. Its musky aroma can also enhance sensuality and passion in spells geared toward lust, attraction, and love as well as help you manifest your desires and attract wealth and prosperity.

Peppermint

Peppermint essential oil's cooling and stimulating scent can help you feel more alert and energized, not to mention that one whiff can help with headaches, nausea, digestion, and respiratory issues. So it's clearly one of the more potent magickal ingredients out there. But peppermint oil can also be used in spells for cleansing, protection, prosperity, releasing negativity, and encouraging lucid dreaming.

MAKING INFUSED OILS

Making essential oils usually involves special machinery, which is why it's cheaper and easier to buy them ready-made. But *infused* oils are just as magickal and far less of a pain to DIY. You simply add your herbs and flowers to a Mason jar, top them with a plant-based oil (such as olive or sunflower), let steep for a few days, and then strain the liquid into a (preferably dark glass) vial.

Rosemary

Rosemary essential oil is a powerful and aromatic oil often used for healing, purification, love, and protection. It's especially useful in binding and cleansing spells or in rituals that require clarity and communication.

A Magickal Goody Bag

Ready to put all of these magickal components together and create something powerful? If you are someone who likes a physical reminder of your intention, keeping a small bag of components in your pocket (or even your bra) is a great way to do that. In Hoodoo, it would be called a "mojo bag." But since we're not following a specific practice here, "goody bag" is just fine. The spirits of the herbs, essential oils, amulets, crystals, and your intention will vibe together as one, amplifying the charm's energy.

YOU'LL NEED:

- An herb aligned with your intention
- A clear quartz crystal to amplify your intention
- Any small charms that may be helpful (e.g., a four-leaf clover to bring you luck or a dandelion seed to manifest your intention)
- A few strands of your hair
- Your intention, written on a piece of paper
- A small pouch
- A tealight
- An essential oil aligned with your intention

1. Gather all of your components in your hands. Breathe gently on them until you feel like the components have aligned with your intention, then carefully add them to the bag.

2. Holding your intention, mindfully light the tealight. Gently run the bag above the flame (being careful not to set anything on fire) until you feel like its tiny spirit is waking up.

3. Whisper your intention to the bag and anoint it with essential oil. Then extinguish the tealight. Slip the bag into your pocket (or wherever you prefer) and carry it with you.

4. When it feels like your charm bag has run out of charge, bury it in a bowl of salt placed on the windowsill overnight and then repeat running it over the flame of a tealight while holding your intention. If you feel like the goody bag's work is done and it's accomplished what it was intended to do, you can thank it and disassemble it.

Hot Tip

Because this is really personal magick that you will be keeping physically close to you (and mingling with your energy), you want to be sure to keep it safe. If someone with bad intentions found your goody bag, they could stir up all kinds of nasty business with it.

Light Your Fire with Candle Magick

Candle magick is a vital part of any witchcraft tool kit—especially for broke witches. It's inexpensive, it doesn't require a lot of components, and it can be used with any intention. Plus, there's still a little bit of magickal flash to it thanks to the range of colors, scents, and more. You can even anoint candles with essential oils, encrust them in pretty herbs, or center them in crystal chips for a little extra oomph. Until then, a plain white candle lit with intention will do the trick. The light from the candle carries our intention skyward, sending a tiny beacon to the Universe about our intention and helping us connect with the Universe to manifest our witchcraft. (Pretty cool, right?)

Rein It In

We've all seen those witchcraft candles on socials—glorious, giant, heady confections full of glitter, whole herbs, flower petals, big quartz points, multicolored waxes, essential oils, sigils, narwhal tears, and a couple naturally shed unicorn horns thrown in for good measure. They've got gorgeous labels, have been blessed during a full-moon solar eclipse, and are called Sisterhood of the Howling Moon or something like that. Who wouldn't want a candle like that? You don't. I mean, you do. You may even break down and buy a couple. (The Universe knows I have. I have one in a box right now that I don't dare open to even look at.) But try to resist.

You don't need candles that elaborate. And, more importantly, you don't *want* candles that elaborate. First of all, they cost way too much money for something you're going to burn. And that's if you are ever going to actually burn something that beautiful. More likely, you will you just save it for a special occasion that never happens. What coven ritual is ever going to feel special enough for the Sisterhood of the Howling Moon candle?

But let's say you have no problem using nice things with wild abandon. No problem then, right? Wrong. If that candle catches its herbs on fire or explodes, you'll have more to worry about than hot firefighters interrupting your coven ritual (been there). At the very least, you'll be scraping wax off of everything in the room, which is time consuming and annoying (been there too). And when you add a bunch of objects to the kind of glass-encased candles most metaphysical shops sell, explosion is always a possibility. The lesson here: Even when you do add the odd oil or herb to your candle, keep it simple. (And maybe skip the glass-encased candles in favor of putting everything on a fireproof plate.) It'll save you money *and* trouble.

MAKING GORGEOUS WITCHY CANDLES SAFELY

Restraint in your candle making is never a bad thing. Does that mean you can't have gorgeous candles? Of course not. But making these kinds of candles yourself allows you to keep safety in mind, infuse every element with your intention, and save some dough while you're at it.

To add components to a container candle, place the candle in a small pot with enough water so that the waterline is halfway up the candle. Let it simmer over low heat until the top of the candle softens. Then shut off the heat and wait until the candle is cool enough to handle with a potholder. Press your components into the softened wax. Here are some other tips:

- Less is almost always going to be more. If you want to go crazy with the components, you can always put them next to your candle.

- Use permanent marker to make sigils on the outside of the container.

- Use no more than ½ teaspoon total of dried and finely powdered herbs and flowers.

- Use no more than three crystal chips (not whole crystals).

- Use no more than nine drops of essential oil, don't let the oil get near the wick, and let the oil dry before lighting the candle (because oil + flames = bad).

- If you must use glitter, use only the biodegradable kind, and no more than ½ teaspoon.

Add Some Color

While you can use a white candle for any ritual or intention, you can also supercharge your magick by choosing a candle in a color that aligns with your intention.

- **BLACK** for protection, release, removing negativity, unblocking your chakras, and invoking Saturn vibes

- **WHITE** for purification and connecting to the Universe

- **SILVER** for stability, divination work, connecting to your will, and invoking Moon vibes

- **GOLD** for success, confidence, acquiring wealth, and invoking Sun vibes

- **PINK** for mental wellness and love in all its forms (including self-love)

- **PURPLE** for healing, wisdom, empowerment, protection of the home, and invoking Mercury vibes

- **BLUE** for career stability, peace, restful sleep, and invoking Jupiter vibes

- **GREEN** for money, abundance, luck, and invoking Venus vibes

- **YELLOW** for communication, creativity, and learning

- **ORANGE** for new beginnings, strength, and transformation

- **RED** for passion, courage, spicy feelings, and invoking Mars vibes

Size Matters (Sometimes)

You can use whatever candles you have on hand, from a plain white tealight to that three-wick candle you keep forgetting to burn. But many spells are strengthened by letting the candle burn out on its own. If you're short on time or unable to supervise your flame, opt for the tealight or even a birthday candle. But you can also buy inexpensive batches of spell candles (also called "chime candles"), which are small, come in a variety of colors, and burn for just a couple of hours.

Using Sigils

Sigil magick is a really easy, powerful, and totally free way to boost your intention when working with candle magick. It's basically a shorthand version of your intention, written as one cohesive symbol. You just need a pencil, some scratch paper, and a few minutes to create one.

- Using positive language, distill your intention down to one short phrase or sentence. For example, "I trust my body." Write it down.

- Cross out the vowels and any consonants that repeat so you have just a handful of letters. (In my example, this would look like "trsmybd.") These are basically a bunch of arcs and lines that you can combine into a symbol infused with your intention.

- Arrange the remaining letters into a sigil formation that you like. One way of doing this is to write the letters in a circle and draw lines to each letter. But if you're artistically inclined, you can get a little creative with how you incorporate and connect the letters.

- Once you have your sigil, inscribe it in some way on your candle. You can use a permanent marker to draw it onto the candle's container, sketch it onto a small piece of paper and tape it to the bottom of the candle, decoupage it onto the candle with crepe paper, or just carve it right into the wax using a toothpick—whatever works for you.

- Focus again on your intention. Lick your fingertip (your saliva is a physical manifestation of your will) and touch your fingertip to the sigil to activate the sigil and align it with your intention.

WORTH *the* SPLURGE

Once you have a little more wiggle room in your budget, you can invest in a few pricey-but-powerful materials. Here are some suggestions:

Spendy Essential Oils

Depending on the main ingredient, some essential oils may be pricier than others. The following oils fall into that category but are worth splurging on.

- **Bergamot** for money, joy, and success
- **Rose Otto** for love in all its forms (you can use rose water as a substitute while you're saving up)
- **Sandalwood** for calmness and connecting with spirits, ancestors, and goddesses

Organic Candles

If all you can find or afford are paraffin candles, that's OK! But candles made from organic materials like beeswax or soy can be worth the added investment. Not only are they better for the environment and safer to take deep breaths around, they also enhance your connection to the natural world.

Sealing Wax

Fun as they may be (especially if you're a crafter by nature), you don't need elaborate sealing-wax kits to perform magick. But owning at least one stick of sealing wax is useful for certain spells—particularly spell jars. White is a great starting point, but you can also find inexpensive bundles of assorted colors. And you typically use only a little bit at a time, which makes sealing wax an economical addition to your practice.

Create Your Own Ritual Candle

Ready to put all of the components together and make the magick happen? Make this ritual your own by mixing and matching whatever you have on hand or whatever calls to you in the moment. Consider your options: What color candle would be best? Which essential oil or oil blend would work well with your intention? Which crystals would work best? Be mindful about the objects you choose. And if you're just dipping your toes into the magickal waters, skip the herbs, oils, and crystals altogether and stick with just the candle and the sigil. Sometimes the simple spells are the best ones!

YOU'LL NEED:

- A candle (white, or whichever color aligns with your intention)
- A sigil of your intention
- Dried herbs aligned with your intention
- An essential oil aligned with your intention
- Crystals or crystal chips aligned with your intention
- Any additional components that hold meaning for you
- A metal lid from a jar or a candle snuffer

1. Focus on your intention while adding your sigil and any herbs, oils, or crystals to or around your candle (using the previously mentioned safety precautions).

2. When you're ready, hold your hands over the candle and let your intention flow through them.

3. Put your candle somewhere that's firesafe (this doesn't have to be an altar—even the kitchen sink will do). As you light the candle, say: *With this flame, I ignite my wish's true aim. Let my will be a bonfire for all that I desire. And so it is.*

4. Let the candle burn down completely. If you need to extinguish the candle, do so with a metal jar lid or a candle snuffer after thanking the flame's spirit. Then relight it daily, while focusing on your intention, until it's burnt out.

Hot Tip

You can also tie magickal objects around the candle. Yarn, an amulet, feathers, ribbon—if it has meaning to you or your spell, it's worth including. (But if you tie them to the candle itself and not a container, make sure you remove them before the flame gets too close.)

You just have to
get clear on what
you really want.

CHAPTER 3

Your Inner Terrarium

Mind, Body, and Spirit

We all know about the mind-body connection, right? We know that stress can give people heart attacks, for example. But, more and more, people are realizing that spirituality (in whatever form you recognize it) is also part of that equation. It could be feeling peaceful at the end of a yoga class when *namaste* is said, or being in the woods and vibing with nature, or feeling energized and empowered by helping others. You get to decide how that spiritual connection manifests in your practice—whether it's as the breath of the Universe; the will of your goddesses, ancestors, and spirits; or the stardust in your veins.

However you connect with your spirituality, it's a sacred part of you. And that makes it essential to your witchcraft. That relationship between mind, body, and spirit—your Sacred Three—is the foundation of your magickal practice. It connects you with the Universe, gives you purpose, and makes your magick more powerful and potent. And—bonus—it doesn't cost a thing! But it does mean getting your internal house (your inner terrarium) in order.

BE YOUR MOST *INTENTIONAL* SELF

A phrase that gets thrown around a lot in reference to the mind/body/spirit connection is "your authentic self." People love to go on and on about how important it is to be true to your authentic self. Strongly disagree. Why? Your most authentic self is a self-involved jerk. It's full of all your crummiest factory settings and impulses. Your most authentic self—the inner primate that underlies all of humanity—just cares about surviving. Does that sound like a witch who is connected to her Sacred Three? Does that sound like a witch who is focused on his intention and all the magickal and practical work needed to get to it? No. It does not. You are more than your factory settings, and what you do every day as a witch centers you in your connection to what you are building for yourself with your sacred intention. In other words, you want to be better than your most authentic self. You want to be your most *intentional* self.

Uncovering Faulty Connections

So how do you connect these three aspects of yourself? First, figure out whether you feel a disconnection anywhere. Do you feel present in your body, but your brain is screaming and your spirit is out to lunch? Do you feel like your spirit is vibing with the Universe and your brain is on point, but your body makes you feel like you're living with an unhappy roommate? Maybe you're just endlessly scrolling through your socials and avoiding certain aspects of your thoughts, feelings, and physical state. Journaling can help you sort things out and find balance. (No, this is not an excuse to buy yet another cute notebook. A spare piece of paper will do.) Use the following prompts to check in with yourself.

- Do I feel stressed out and overwhelmed more often than I feel calm and content?

- Am I fulfilling my daily tasks without too much strain? If I'm feeling strained, what's causing it?

- Do I feel disconnected from certain feelings? Why?

- Do I feel comfortable in my body? Why or why not?

- Have I been avoiding movement with my body? Why or why not?

- Have I been eating things that make me feel good? Why or why not?

- Have I been feeding my spirit with things like meditation, time outside, journaling, helping others, and spiritual contemplation? Why or why not?

- Do I feel more aware of my gratitude or my hardships? Why?

- Does my spirit/psyche feel centered? Why or why not?

Take a deep breath and look over your answers. Do you notice a pattern? A specific area of disconnection? There are probably some aspects of your sacred self that are ready for repair.

Repair can come in big and small changes; it's up to you to decide what's right for you. Take a moment to brainstorm ways that might make you feel more connected with the parts of you that need it most. Maybe you want to go to therapy to deal with past issues, start a gratitude practice, or begin journaling daily. Or maybe you decide to take yoga, cut out certain not-so-healthy foods, and eat more fruits and vegetables. No matter what you choose to do to create that connection, there's one thing that can help: committing to being more present.

Being Present

Being present can be incredibly difficult, but it is one of the fastest ways to align your three sacred aspects. It keeps you from getting stuck in the past, worrying about the future, or being distracted from what's really important. Obviously, it's not something we can do all the time, but the more you practice, the easier it gets.

Being present requires you to be engaged with what's happening in that moment. If you are at dinner with a loved one, it means concentrating on the food and connecting with the other person. If you are feeling stressed out at work, it means sitting with that feeling and trying to work your way through it instead of stress-eating stale cake in the breakroom. If you are trying to sleep, and your mind is whirling like a hamster on a wheel, it means concentrating on your breath. In other words, being present allows you to notice and provide what your mind, body, and spirit need in the moment.

None of us will ever be perfect at this—the world is full of delicious, interesting, exciting distractions. It's OK to get a little distracted sometimes, whether it's by engaging in a juicy text sesh, playing a world-building video game, or learning how to make a perfect latte. It makes life fun. But making the effort to be more present with your daily life will help you tend to your Sacred Three. And that, in turn, will help you be more attuned to your witchcraft. If that's not enough of a selling point, it will also help you feel more fulfilled every day. (That's the goal, at least!)

A Crystal Rite for Manifesting Connection

Crystal grids are energetically charged geometric patterns on which you place crystals to feed off of each other and amplify each other's magick, and they can be a great help in connecting your Sacred Three. In general, crystal grids can be as free-form or structured as you like. You can use predesigned ones, or you can create your own patterns. For this ritual, you're going to use the Seed of Life grid, which symbolizes balance and harmony. (A quick Google search will help you find one you can print out, or you can draw your own on a sheet of paper. In this case, size doesn't matter.)

YOU'LL NEED:

- A printout or drawing of a Seed of Life pattern
- 13 crystals:
  - 1 clear quartz to amplify your intention
- 6 rose quartz for self-love
- 6 amethyst for healing and clarity

1. Lay your grid on a flat surface (like your altar, if you have one). Focus on your intention to reconnect your Sacred Three aspects.

2. Place the rose quartz crystals on the outer ring of the grid, where the inner circles meet the outer circles. Then place the amethyst crystals at the outer points of the flower in the center of the pattern. Finally, place the clear quartz crystal at the center of the flower.

3. Use your index finger like a wand to activate the grid by touching the crystals, moving from the rose quartz and amethyst crystals to the clear quartz to connect them.

4. Focus on your intention while gazing at the center point. When you feel like your intention has been aligned with the center point, exhale deeply and lift your intention to the stars.

5. Seal your work by saying: *I align with my Sacred Three.* So I will it, so let it be. Leave the stones in place for a full moon cycle (thirty days).

Once you finish the ritual, you can move the stones or change them out every thirty days, depending on what you feel you need to be part of the grid.

Hot Tip

You can use inexpensive crystal chips instead of larger crystals to save both money and space.

Getting Centered

Once you find balance between your Sacred Three, you need to learn how maintain it—especially during stressful situations that can pack a punch to your energy. That doesn't mean you always need to be happy or never get upset like some kind of robot. It just means that you don't allow yourself to be driven by your emotions. Taking charge of your emotions can help you stay centered during difficulties in life, which will also keep you centered in your witchcraft. (And that's important if you don't want any wayward hexes wreaking havoc.) But the opposite is also true. For example, if you are a barista and you are slammed at work with a lot of complicated orders from grumpy customers, being able to ground and center yourself through the techniques you've been practicing as a witch (like the one on page 32) can help keep you from burning yourself with hot espresso . . . or throwing it at the grumpy customers.

WORK SMARTER

You can use the skills you've been learning and practicing as a witch to make your life at work easier. A little honey-pot spell for good tips, a glamour spell so that customers and coworkers find you perfectly *charming*, and a grounding ritual during your break are all great options.

Creating a Sacred Scent for Centering

It's easy to go through life just reacting to whatever's going on around us rather than striving to be our best, most intentional self. Even when you do commit to grounding and centering yourself, some days you'll still let your emotions take the wheel. We all do. But that commitment helps you rebalance your Sacred Three no matter how stressed or annoyed you are in the moment. One more thing that can help? Scent. In addition to each aroma's magickal properties, scent itself helps you focus inward in the moment and recalibrate. Let's create a sacred scent to remind yourself that you are a witch who lives with centered intention.

YOU'LL NEED:

- A rollerball perfume bottle or other small vessel
- A few dried lavender buds for grounding and centering
- A tiny piece of dried lemon peel for focus
- A tiny sprig of cedar for success

- 3 citrine crystal chips for joy, confidence, and success
- 3 drops lavender essential oil
- 3 drops lemon essential oil
- 3 drops cedar essential oil
- Grapeseed oil

DO THIS:

1. Focus on your intention to center yourself. Put the buds, peel, cedar, and citrine in your hand and breathe your intention into them.

2. When the components feel infused with your desire, add them to the bottle along with the essential oils.

3. Fill the bottle the rest of the way with grapeseed oil.

4. As you seal the bottle, say: *I am centered, I am grounded, I am focused on my intention. And so it is.*

Setting Your Intention

Understanding and working on your mind/body/ spirit connection is essential to setting intentions in your practice. When your Sacred Three are connected and fulfilled, you can get to the heart of what it is you want. And that helps you set clearer, more effective intentions. You know what doesn't help? A pricey crystal obelisk. Sure, magickal objects can help you amplify your intentions. But you have to do the inner work to understand yourself and your goals before you get quartz involved.

Don't get me wrong, you can do witchcraft for the sheer joy of doing it—the wind in your hair, the feel of the damp earth beneath your bare feet, the ecstatic feeling of drumming or dancing or chanting, the smell of a bonfire. You can do it because it makes you feel free for a moment, whether you are skyclad (naked) and freed of society's expectations, or you're feeling aligned with your coven as you howl at the moon together, or you feel especially in sync with the forest that day. Maybe you just take satisfaction in the scent of a simmer pot, the feeling of shuffling your Tarot deck, the flicker of a candle, or the sound of a witchy song. Finding joy in these things makes you a witch just as much as doing deeply focused witchcraft does. But we all have moments where we want or need something more—that new job, to find romantic partner(s), to heal a wound (emotional or physical), to find creative success, to have more money, or to feel good about ourselves. Whatever it is for you, big or small, putting your witchcraft to work with an intention will empower you, bring you closer to your heart's desire, and keep you motivated to do the work that witchcraft requires. We've already touched on the subject of intention—and maybe you've already done a spell or two (or five)—but considering that your intention drives your magick (and your spending), it's worth a deeper dive.

If you set an intention to meditate for ten minutes every day, spending money on a super fancy meditation cushion, essential oil blends, and a meditation workshop isn't going to make you show up for yourself for that ten-minute block. Those things *could* help, but if you don't actually *do the thing*, then all you did was scratch the shopping itch. Just like you can buy a thousand crystals, but if you never use them for witchcraft, all you have is a room full of expensive rocks. Do the work. *Then* you can sprinkle in a little intentional spending to boost your results.

Getting Clear and Creative

What do you want? That seems like an easy enough question, right? But setting an intention requires you to fully understand that intention—what feelings and desires are behind it, what the consequences might be, how much work it requires, and so on. Let's say you want more money (who doesn't, right?). Well, what does that mean to you? Does it mean finding a couple pennies on the street or having a certain amount in your savings account? Does it mean being able to buy a dress you want or having a vault full of gold coins for you to swim in like Scrooge McDuck? Does it mean winning the lottery or finding a job in your field that pays more? It's all doable (although the swimming pool full of money feels like a health hazard). You just have to get clear on what you *really* want.

For one thing, manifesting a couple pennies on the street is probably going to be significantly easier than manifesting a swimming pool's worth. How much work are you willing to put in? How long are you willing to wait? For another, it's easy to get bogged down by what you *should* want (world peace or whatever) or what you feel you deserve (a modest amount in your savings account). But one of the things that makes witchcraft so exciting is that you can always try manifesting *more*. That savings-account balance

you have in mind? Add another zero to it. Why not? The worst thing that can happen is it doesn't happen. Or you could get the original amount you had in mind. But you could also manifest that extra zero!

No matter what you hope to conjure up with your intention, you want to leave a little wiggle room for the Universe to get creative. If your spell is too tightly worded (and wound), it can limit its effectiveness and even cheat you out of some pretty awesome results you hadn't considered. For example, if your spell to attract a partner includes height, hair color, income, career field, favorite bands, and preferred candy flavors, you could be waiting a really long time for the Universe to find someone who fits the bill. Plus, you're not giving the Universe the option to find someone who would be an amazing fit for you but who happens to like salty more than sweet. You want enough clarity in your intention that the Universe has something to go on, but not so much structure that you don't give her room to play.

Following Through

Knowing your intention is only half the battle. You can't just think something into existence. To set your intention is to state what you intend to accomplish through words, actions, and witchcraft. You are making a commitment to yourself and to the Universe that you are willing to do all the hard work of bringing your intention to life—both through witchcraft and day-to-day life—and not just the fun parts. You are dedicating yourself to *the process*, which will include both exhilarating high points and difficult potholes along the way. You are keeping yourself focused on what your intention will require right now as well as how that thread will eventually weave together with future threads. Combining intention with action is what gets you results.

Controlling Your Will

Your will is your desire for something to happen, but it also refers to your ability to decide to initiate an action. In other words, you need to take practical (and magickal) steps to make things happen. Yes, some witches will have an easier time connecting to their witchcraft than other witches will. Further, having natural talent won't get you very far without discipline and action. You have to cultivate your ability as a witch through practice.

But how do you control your will? When it comes to witchcraft, delayed gratification is key. You won't see the results of your magick right away, so you have to have faith and keep moving forward. What that means is devoting time to practicing your witchcraft every day, even when you could be scrolling through your socials, watching *Real Housewives*, or eating a bag of potato chips. Dedicating yourself to improving your craft in general can help you with the intentions you've set, so it's all upside. All those other things? Very unlikely to bring you closer to getting what you really want. Keep your eyes on the prize.

Planting a Seed of Intention

You don't need a full witch's garden to practice a little nature magick, but this fulfilling little ritual might make you want one. (And if you do, turn to page 101.) You're going to plant a seed infused with your intention and watch it manifest before your eyes. This exercise helps you understand the very real impact your intentions have. You can use this ritual to manifest any intention and know that, as your plant grows, your will is also coming to life. You can use any plant—like cheerful sunflowers or edible herbs—but choosing one that aligns with your intention can give it a boost. Just follow the instructions on the seed packet for best results. (Not even magick can help you with overwatering or leaf scorch.)

YOU'LL NEED:

- A piece of paper
- A pen or pencil
- A small pot
- Dirt or potting soil
- A packet of seeds

DO THIS:

1. Write down your intention, then fold the paper three times toward yourself. Place it at the bottom of the pot.

2. Fill the pot with soil. Open the seed packet and whisper your intention to the seeds before carefully pushing them into the dirt (about ½ inch deep).

3. Place your hands (or fingers) gently on top of the soil and infuse it with your intention.

4. Find a home for the pot in a place where it can get sunlight. Every time you water the soil (the frequency of which depends on the plant), focus on your intention and consider what else you could be doing to manifest it, both magickally and in your daily life.

Hot Tip

Don't get stressed out if your seed doesn't immediately take root and grow—some intentions take more time to manifest than others. If a few weeks go by without any growth, you can always try planting more or different seeds or slightly adjust your intention. (It's also not the worst idea, if your thumb is less than green, to pick an herb that's not just aligned with your intention but also grows easily. I recommend basil, mint, dill, or parsley.)

Inner Sanctum Visualization Ritual

In the next chapter, we'll work on carving out sacred spaces. But you can actually create a sacred space within yourself, too. And while your physical space may be constrained by things like money and location, your inner sanctum doesn't have to be. This is where your imagination gets to go wild. Have you always dreamed of having a meditation pool? A floor-to-ceiling library with wheeled ladders? A dedicated altar? Now's your chance! This visualization ritual doesn't require anything but a few moments of your time and doesn't cost a thing, but it has a powerful impact on your magick.

This ritual can help you realign your Sacred Three when you start to feel out of whack by providing you with a calming internal space, like a touchpoint to which you can return. You can use this space to reflect on any feelings of disconnection, or you can even ask your goddesses, ancestors, and nature spirits to visit you there and provide guidance. And because it takes discipline to create and maintain your inner sanctum, doing so will help strengthen the rest of your magickal practice. Use this practice when you first wake up or before you go to sleep—when you're least distracted by life—for the greatest impact.

DO THIS:

1. Sit comfortably in a quiet space. Breathe in through your nose and out through your mouth. Keep doing this until you feel present in your body and your brain isn't screaming distractions at you. (It's OK if a distracting thought or feeling comes up. It's weirder if it doesn't. The goal is to be at least mostly present in your body, not tangled up in thinking about who said what to whom at lunch.) This could take just a moment, or it could take longer. Be patient with yourself.

2. If it feels right to you, close your eyes. Imagine yourself walking down a spiral staircase. Try to visualize as many details as you can. What are the stairs made of? What kind of shoes are you wearing? Are you moving slowly or quickly? Are the stairs lit by candlelight or big sunny windows?

3. When you reach the bottom of the staircase, there will be a door. What does the door look like? What does the doorknob look like? Open the door. What do you see and experience? What does the landscape or room look like? Take a moment to really take it in. Touch, smell, listen, look, taste. Look for the right place to build your inner sanctum, continuing to move through the space until you find it.

4. Once you find the perfect spot, think about what you want your sanctum to look like. (You don't need to worry about anyone else's comfort but your own.) Will it be big or small? How many rooms will it have, and what will each be? What's the color scheme? Do you have rugs or hardwood flooring? What materials is your furniture made out of?

5. Next, think about how you'll use the space. Where will you do rituals? What do you need to be able to do a ritual? Do you have any special things in your space, such as an antique mirror or a clawfoot bathtub? Do you keep food or books in your space? Keep going until you can visualize every detail.

Spend as much time as you need building this space for yourself. If it takes you a few sessions, that's fine too. Just follow the staircase to the door to enter your space. Keep giving yourself time and space to develop this sanctum for yourself, even after you've filled it out. The more you interact with it and make it your own, the more it will be able to act as a safe space for yourself in your magickal practice.

Hot Tip

You can also do things in your physical space to solidify your inner-sanctum visualization, such as drawing the space, building a mini version of it, creating a mood board for it, or journaling about it.

It's the belief,
the intention,
that makes a
space sacred.

CHAPTER 4

Sacred Spaces

What Makes a Space Sacred?

Historically, there were often specific rites and rituals that made a place sacred—think Stonehenge, St. Patrick's Cathedral, the Temple Mount, and so on. The words, the rituals, and the spiritual intention may be different from place to place, but what links all of them is that people view them as holy, worthy of respect and dedication. It's the belief, the *intention*, that makes a space sacred, not the space itself.

Thankfully, that lowers the bar on what can become a sacred space for witches who maybe don't have the space or budget to create a whole temple devoted to their craft. All you really need is a little energetic haven for yourself. (Being able to keep all your witchy stuff in one place is a bonus.) It could be an underutilized closet, a spare bedroom, a corner of your own bedroom, or even just a dedicated shelf. And the possibility for sacred spaces doesn't stop at your front door. Your yard and even local spots where you feel a spiritual connection count, too.

THE MOBILE SACRED SPACE

Does declaring a sacred space mean that you can't do magick anywhere else? Of course not. That would be super limiting. Plus, there are practical considerations. Generally speaking, it's a good idea to have access to water if you're working with fire. And if you are doing a bathing ritual, you'll probably want to do it in the bathroom. Your magick needs to go where you do. Luckily, all you need to make a space sacred for a moment in time is the intention to do so.

Making Room for Magick

If you were a somewhat wealthy person living in medieval times, your closet wasn't a place to haphazardly toss an assortment of clothes, shoes, and holiday decor. It was a place to admire carefully displayed treasured possessions. You might even read, spend time in contemplation, and engage in your spiritual activities there.

This practice is gaining popularity again today through social media, where people are showing off closets repurposed as reading nooks, offices, and more. If you are very crafty, you could turn a closet into a pretty tricked-out ritual space for yourself. But there's no need to turn your search for sacred space into a DIY project. Consider where in your house might a good space for you to do ritual work. Even if your space is limited, you probably have more options than you think.

Form Is Function

In witchcraft as in architecture, it's never a bad idea to make decisions primarily based on functionality and then worry about form (those pretty—and often pricey—touches) later. It makes sense, spiritually and practically, for practicing witches to carve out a sacred space for their spellwork. And it's more important for the space to function well than to look like a perfect, Pinterest-worthy version of a witch's home. You could have the most beautifully arranged altar or ritual space, but if it doesn't serve your intention, it doesn't serve you. So, first and foremost, think about what you want and need out of your sacred space—especially what kinds of spells your practice will include—before you knock down any walls or hit the stores for witchy decor.

Rethink Existing Spaces

Once you know what you want from your practice, you can think about the best space for it. And that might be a space that's already in use. Are there spaces in your home that attract clutter? What about spaces that are full of good intentions and bad follow-through? (Like that craft project you've been meaning to get to, the stack of books you keep meaning to read, and the pile of clothes that need to be repaired.) You have two options: do the thing—now—or move those items along to their next adventures by donating them, recycling them, or gifting them to someone who will actually use them. Either way, those items are taking up space that you could potentially repurpose for your practice.

Curate Your Home's Energy

Another totally free yet powerful practice is paying attention to your space's energy. While you can create a magickally conducive energy in any dedicated space, you want your whole home to feel good. For one thing, you don't always know where your magick will take you from day to day—like from the altar in your spare room to the kitchen. For another, your living space can amplify or detract from your magick. So do what you can to make sure it fuels you.

What gives you that energetic charge is unique to you, so you have to take a look around and decide what adds to your energy and what drains it. In this age of cloud storage, you don't *need* books. But if books are important to you, you'll want to allocate space for them in your home (however tiny and cozy it may be). Maybe you don't repurpose your closet because your beautifully arranged shoes make you happy. And maybe you add some inexpensive witchy touches to existing spaces, like lining your drawer with thrifted velvet or painting your train case with meaningful sigils. It's good for both your magick and your mental health to curate your space. But if that pile of unused cast-iron cookware you inherited from your great-aunt is taking up valuable space and energy, it's time to donate it and make more room for magick.

DECLUTTERING *is* MAGICK

Just as carving out a space for your witchcraft makes room
for magick, mindful care and decluttering of magickal
components can raise that space's vibe. Keep your witchcraft
stores tidy by tossing out things that have expired, keeping
dishware washed, disposing of incense ash, and so on.

Budget Your Space

Your financial budget isn't the only consideration when you're eyeing up that new cauldron (aka slow cooker) or apothecary box. Maybe you live in a tiny space and you're down to your favorite four mugs, you have your off-season clothes vacuum-sealed under your bed, and you've gone completely digital for all your media. In other words, you're maxed out on stuff. That's all the more reason to be mindful in your witchcraft practice and not buy all the things—even if they're cheap or you can afford them. Before you hit "add to cart," think about where your witchcraft components will live. A dedicated space will not only keep things handy, it will also keep you from mindlessly buying more than you have room for. Another crystal isn't going to make you more of a witch; engaging with your practice will. (That said, a few components that you enjoy aren't going to make you *not* a witch either. But mindfulness is important here.)

If you have limited space, think creatively. Maybe your ritual space can be your bed when you have some time to yourself. Maybe it's a mediation cushion and some fairy lights in a closet. Maybe it's your bathroom with the door closed. Just do what you can with what you have. It'll be enough.

Sacred Space Blessing

Once you've figured out where your rituals will take place and where you will store your components, you'll want to set your intention for the space. Blessing these spaces and declaring them sacred will not only prime them for magick but also keep you from getting lazy and tossing old cell-phone chargers in with your witchcraft components. You can bless your space simply by declaring your intention (see step 5). But if you want a little extra magickal oomph, you can use components aligned with your intention.

Before you dive in, consider what your intention for the space actually is. Is it for housemates to stay out of your (witchcraft) stuff? Is it to be left alone and unbothered during your rites? Is it for you to walk the path of the witch and create powerful magick? Or is it something else altogether? When you have your intention in mind, you can start the ritual.

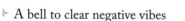

YOU'LL NEED:

- A bell to clear negative vibes
- Prepared mug of ginger tea for strengthening your power
- Frankincense incense stick for purification
- Sea salt for protection
- Amethyst chips for blessings
- Cedar chips for consecration
- A small bowl

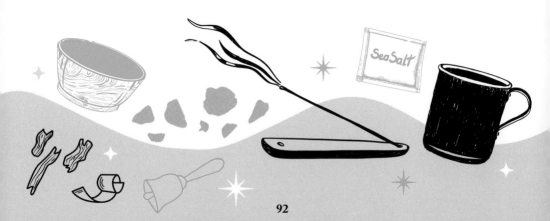

Sea Salt

1. Ring the bell to clear out any previous negative energy from the space.

2. Inhale the scent of the ginger tea and drink some while setting your intention for this work.

3. Once you settle into your intention, light the incense and carefully waft the smoke around the space to purify it.

4. Add the sea salt, amethyst, and cedar chips to a small bowl while focusing on your intention. This will be a focal reminder of your intention.

5. Breathe into the space and say: *May my intention for this sacred space be sealed in with my breath. So I will it, so it shall be.*

Altars Big and Small

Altars are a sacred physical space for you to use to manifest your intention because they accumulate energy. They're a common aspect of witchcraft because they provide a focal point and visual reference when practicing. They also act as a mirror, reflecting your witchy self back to you. That makes them a great place to perform rituals, meditate, seek inspiration, and connect with your practice.

Despite the beautifully decorated and arranged altars you see all over social media, not every witch uses an altar. Having one doesn't make you any more of a witch, and not having one doesn't make you less of a witch. Witchcraft is all about doing what feels right to you. As long as you make a thoughtful decision, you're good.

If you do choose to use an altar, you don't need to commit to creating it right this minute. Take your time and consider what you really need from it, and what it needs from you. For example, you probably don't need picture-perfect crystal shelves, extensive collections of potions, and a pricey mortar and pestle to energize your altar. Just keep your altar simple and true to you.

DEDICATED STORAGE SPACE

You don't need an altar, but having a dedicated area to store your witchy components can keep you from turning the house upside down when you need your crystals, herbs, oils, or whatever. And that little bit of organization alone can help you focus on and strengthen your intention.

What Is an Altar Used For?

A better question would probably be *How does your brain work?* How you use an altar is going to depend on your individual magickal practice and preferences. An altar is like a desk—it holds everything you feel you need to do your magickal work and study. (Instead of a laptop and paper clips, it might hold your spellbooks and candles.) So consider how you organize yourself in life when you are working on projects with smaller moving pieces and apply that logic to your altar. Some witches use one altar to do all their witchcraft. Others prefer to dedicate little spaces to different purposes (e.g., one little space for career success, one for protecting their home, one for setting intentions using directional navigation, one for a particular goddess, ancestor, or spirit). There's no right or wrong answer. It's all about figuring out how to align your brain with your witchcraft.

What Do I Even Put on an Altar?

This is where things get tricky for broke witches. When you're creating your altar, the temptation to fill it with pretty things is strong. But if you start by mindfully deciding what kind of practice you want to cultivate, and you tap into your will to create it, you can design an altar that empowers you instead of just looking good. Don't worry, though—even an inexpensive setup can fill you with joy. And there are plenty of ways to save so that you can afford a few fun extras.

First, you want to set your intention for your altar space. Having that in mind will help you figure out what goes where and which components you need. If your altar is going to be all-purpose, consider what objects will do the most for your practice. Things like a bowl of clear quartz and a white candle to amplify your intentions, an espresso cup and saucer for offerings, a small bell to cleanse the space, a bowl of salt to reduce negative energy, a candle snuffer, and a small firesafe bowl would cover a lot of bases in your witchcraft.

Altars are often covered with cloths, as well, but you don't need to buy one for the purpose. Your cloth can be cut from a piece of clothing you love but can no longer wear, a bit of fabric you thrifted, or something you make yourself by knitting, crocheting, or quilting. And deciding not to have an altar cloth is a valid choice too.

If you have multiple altars for different purposes, or you just want to change things out depending on your current focus, you can keep things equally simple. Here are a few examples:

- **MANIFESTING A NEW JOB:** A green altar cloth, a bowl of cedar chips, moonstone and green aventurine crystals, and a tealight with a dab of orange oil on it.

- **STRENGTHENING A RELATIONSHIP:** A pink altar cloth, a bowl of rose petals, rose and clear quartz crystals, and a tealight with a little lemon oil on it.

- **PROTECTING YOUR HOME:** A blue altar cloth, a bowl of salt, dried lavender buds, an amethyst crystal, and a tealight with a few drops of lavender oil.

- **COMMUNING WITH A SPECIFIC GODDESS, SPIRIT, OR ANCESTOR:** A white altar cloth, a small framed picture of the spirit, an offering setting (small plate, small glass, small candle holder), a white candle, and any offerings the spirit would like.

You can even challenge yourself to see how few objects you can use to support your intention—whatever that may be.

BROKE WITCH TIP

Thrift those magickal components! You'd be amazed by how much witchy stuff you can find at secondhand stores—especially now that magick is more mainstream and attention spans are short. Here are a few altar-worthy items to keep an eye out for:

· Multicolored candles

· Candle snuffers

· Chalk for drawing sigils

· Compact mirrors for reflecting energy

· Fabric for altar cloths

· Firesafe vessels for burning herbs and candles

· Glass bottles and jars for potions and components

· Grimoires (journals)

· Offering vessels (dishware)

· Picture frames

· Cauldrons (slow cookers)

· Vintage bells for cleansing

A Tiny, Traveling Elemental Altar

Many practices and rituals involve the use of the elements (earth, air, fire, and water). Luckily, preparing an altar for this kind of work is cheap, easy, and efficient. This tiny altar can fit in the smallest of spaces and go everywhere you go. It relies mostly on found objects, which save you money and foster a connection with the natural world. Just make sure all of your components will fit in your tin with the lid closed. Any spell can benefit from calling on the elements, but this altar is especially useful for rituals involving spirits, goddesses, ancestors, nature, and the Universe.

YOU'LL NEED:

- An empty mint tin
- Cedar essential oil
- A square of fabric to line the tin
- A tealight
- A tiny seashell to represent water
- A tiny stone to represent earth
- A tiny feather to represent air
- A birthday candle to represent fire

- A tiny corked jar filled with:
  - Clear quartz chips for amplifying your intention
  - Salt for grounding
  - Rose petals for love
  - Rosemary for prosperity
  - Lavender for peace
- A jingle bell on a ribbon for cleansing the space
- A compass (or compass app) for determining placement of the elements

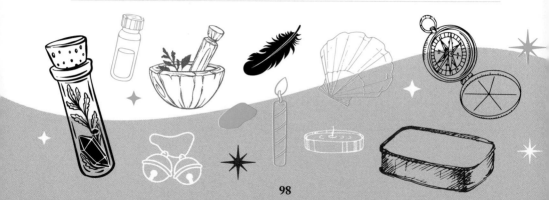

1. Take a deep breath. Focus on your intention to build a tiny sacred space. Dab a few drops of the cedar essential oil onto the tin itself, the lining fabric, and the tealight.

2. When dry, light the tealight so that it's burning while you work. Add the seashell, stone, feather, birthday candle, corked jar, and jingle bell to the tin and close it. Pass the filled tin over the candle.

3. Set up your altar by removing the contents of the tin and laying your altar cloth over the tin. Use your compass to put the elemental items in the correct places: the stone to the north, the feather to the east, the birthday candle to the south, the seashell to the west, and the jar in the center (this represents your connection to the Universe).

4. Ring the jingle bell to make the space sacred while focusing on consecrating your tiny altar.

5. When you're finished, put all the components back into the tin and breathe on (or kiss) the tin to attune your altar with your energy. Then say: *By my breath, by my power, this altar is sacred. So let it be.*

6. To use the altar in the future, simply repeat steps 3 and 4 before beginning your ritual.

Knowing Your (Spirit of) Place

Many witches feel called to witchcraft due to feeling a connection to the natural world around them. The wild animals, the plants, the dirt, the cycles of the moon, the wind, the ocean—one or all of those things call to them. Maybe you are one of those witches, maybe you're not. Maybe the idea of camping gives you hives, you live in a big city, or you've just never thought about it much. But in addition to strengthening your magick, exploring a connection with nature is generally a pretty inexpensive venture. And it can start with the mini forest of trees near your house, a local park, your backyard, or even your little apartment balcony.

Your Genius Loci

One way to connect with nature is to connect with your *genius loci*, which means "the spirit of a place." It can refer both to natural places you vibe with and to the actual guardian spirit of a place. Fostering your connection with your genius loci is not only low cost, it's also good for your magick. You connect with your genius loci by interacting with and observing it. You might document the cycles of nature, plant protective herbs, eat locally, help care for feral cats in your neighborhood, or go for walks in the park every week. When you slow down and pay attention, you will notice all kinds of things about your habitat. These moments connect you to the land as a witch, which pays dividends in your practice. All of that energy you generate and interact with gets infused into your magick, and your genius loci may even reward your effort with magick of its own.

Feeling Grounded in the City

It's easy to forget about nature when you live in a bustling city, but it's still there! There's still wildlife, plants, bodies of water, and sky. There are other natural things that are special to city life, too: rooftop gardens, botanical parks, historical grounds, and skyline walks with lush greenery. And the cycles of nature will still be there for you to connect with. You just have to take notice.

The Witch's Garden

Gardening is part of many a magickal practice, which makes sense when you consider witchcraft's deep roots in nature. And it's another opportunity to create sacred spaces. In addition to strengthening your spiritual connection with your genius loci, getting your hands dirty helps you infuse your magickal components with intention and energy, giving your spellwork an extra boost. And although there's no shame in grabbing your herbs at the grocery store, growing your own may be easier and more economical than you think. Whether you have access to a sprawling yard, a cute English garden, an apartment balcony, or a sunny windowsill, you can embrace your inner green witch and save some money at the same time.

Planning Your Magickal Haven

First things first: planning. Before you dive into the earth and start planting, take a moment to envision your dream garden. Consider the available space, sunlight exposure, and types of plants you want to cultivate. And make sure you align your choices with your intention. Are you drawn to protection, love, prosperity, or divination? Choose plants that resonate with your magickal goals.

From Seed to Spell

One of the most rewarding aspects of gardening is propagating your plants. Instead of buying slightly pricier starter plants, why not start from seed and infuse your garden with your own magickal intention? Here's a quick how-to:

- **SELECTING SEEDS:** Choose organic, non-GMO seeds that align with your magickal intention. Basil, lavender, rosemary, and thyme are some of the easiest and most powerful options.

- **GERMINATION:** Hold the seeds in your left hand and breathe a blessing over them. You can say something like, "May this breath help you reach your fullest potential." Then follow the planting and care instructions on the seed packets, making sure you create a nurturing environment with gentle warmth, natural light, and adequate moisture.

- **TENDING TO SEEDLINGS:** As your seedlings emerge, you can offer them more than sunlight and water. Sing to them, talk to them, and continue infusing them with your intention.

- **TRANSPLANTING:** When your seedlings are about 6 inches tall, it's time to transplant them into your garden beds or containers. As you replant them, you can say another blessing or just hold your intention.

- **HARVESTING:** Wait to take cuttings from your plants until they've grown strong and have plenty to spare. And always thank the plant for its contribution when you do.

Don't get discouraged if your seeds don't grow as well as you'd hoped (or at all). Some seeds are duds. Some days are harsher on plants than others. Gardening is full of lessons in will, patience, and letting the Universe take the wheel.

SMALL-SPACE HERBALISM

One way to save money is to DIY your own dried herbs and flowers for teas and potions. If you have limited space, just get creative. A hanger and some breathing room in the closet works just fine.

Miniature Magickal Gardens (Container Planting)

If you have limited space or want to cultivate a portable magickal oasis of greenery, container gardening is the way to go. Here are some tips to create a captivating mini garden:

- **CHOOSING CONTAINERS:** Pretty much anything can be a container as long as it offers room for the plant to grow. Consider thrifting tins, pots, buckets, or even cups and mugs that make you smile. (These are especially great for windowsill herb gardens.)

- **POTTING MIX:** This is one area where you don't want to skimp to save a buck. Fill your containers with a good-quality potting mix. This is the foundation for your plants and your intention.

- **SELECTING PLANTS:** Choose magickal plants that thrive in containers—culinary herbs are perfect for small pots, and you can grow beautiful roses and lemons in larger ones.

- **CARE AND FEEDING:** When it comes to things like pest control and plant food, you can find plenty of cheap, organic, DIY options online. Just set your intention (e.g., to keep your plants safe and happy) as you mix them up and use them.

Magickal Plant Profiles

Now that you know the basics for creating the witch's garden of your dreams (and your reality), you can start planting or propagating your picks. Here are a few tips to get you going with some of the most common (and easy to grow) magickal plants. Just remember to hold your intention for the seeds or cuttings in your mind while you work with them, focusing on amplifying their intrinsic magickal properties. Every time you plant, water, or cut one, you have the opportunity to add some oomph to your future spells.

Basil
Ocimum basilicum

USE ME IN SPELLS FOR: Love, luck, wealth, and protection.

PLANT ME: In loamy, well-draining soil that is rich in organic matter.

WATER ME: Regularly and just enough to keep the soil moist but not soggy.

GIVE ME: Full sun for 6 to 8 hours per day (but some shade in very hot climates).

NOTES: There are numerous varieties of basil, including sweet basil, lemon basil, cinnamon basil, and purple basil. Not only is basil tasty on pizza, it also has medicinal properties.

Chamomile
Matricaria chamomilla

USE ME IN SPELLS FOR: Luck, money, dreams, love, healing, and protection.

PLANT ME: In rich soil with a pH between 5.6 and 7.5.

WATER ME: Moderately and evenly, with care not to over- or under-water.

GIVE ME: Full sun to partial shade.

NOTES: Although this plant is soothing to humans, it's highly toxic to our furry friends.

Lavender

Lavandula angustifolia

USE ME IN SPELLS FOR: Love, sleep, protection, purification, calm, and happiness.

PLANT ME: In well-draining soil after the last frost (or indoors).

WATER ME: Regularly and just enough to keep the soil moist but not damp. Good drainage is key.

GIVE ME: Full sun.

NOTES: Lavender is said to bring happiness to any home that grows it. But it has very unhappy effects on dogs and cats who ingest it, so keep this plant and its potions away from furry family members.

Mint

Mentha

USE ME IN SPELLS FOR: Healing, communication, abundance, luck, love, protection, and clarity.

PLANT ME: In containers to keep me from taking over the garden.

WATER ME: Regularly and enough to keep the soil damp but not waterlogged.

GIVE ME: Partial to full sun.

NOTES: Fresh mint is the perfect addition to any altar, attracting aid from helpful spirits. If you have a sunny spot on your altar, consider growing this herb there.

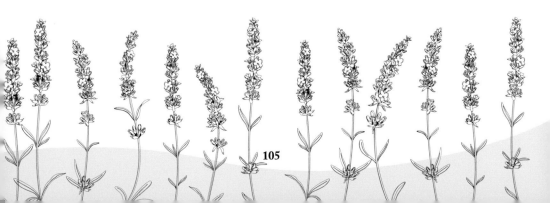

Rosemary

Rosmarinus officinalis

USE ME IN SPELLS FOR: Protection, purification, love, and clarity.

PLANT ME: In well-draining soil with a pH of 6.0 to 7.5.

WATER ME: Deeply but infrequently, and only when the top of the soil is dry.

GIVE ME: Full sun for at least 6 hours a day.

NOTES: Rosemary has been used for protection and purification for centuries, which is why folklore tells us to keep some by our front door or garden gate.

Sage

Salvia officinalis

USE ME IN SPELLS FOR: Protection, wisdom, prosperity, and cleansing.

PLANT ME: In well-draining soil when the temperature reaches 60°F or above.

WATER ME: Infrequently and only when the soil is completely dry.

GIVE ME: Full sun.

NOTES: Common sage has protective properties that make it a must-have for any witch's garden. It acts like a magickal guard dog for your home and land.

Thyme

Thymus vulgaris

USE ME IN SPELLS FOR: Courage, purification, healing, and love.

PLANT ME: In slightly alkaline, well-draining soil.

WATER ME: When the top of the soil has dried.

GIVE ME: Full sun to partial shade.

NOTES: Thyme is a versatile culinary herb known for its medicinal uses—including its antibacterial, anti-inflammatory, and antifungal properties—as much as for its delicious flavor.

Planting a Mini Witch's Garden

You don't need anything fancy to start your witch's garden—a few washed pasta jars, a grocery-store herb bundle, a sunny window, and some intention will do the trick. Just follow the instructions on page 103 to get your herbs ready for transplant. Like most things in magick, growing roots takes time, so plan accordingly. (If you don't have the patience to wait, you're probably not going to love gardening. There's no shame in buying dried herbs.)

A handful of stones (found or purchased) at the bottom of each jar gives your garden the drainage it needs to thrive. To amplify your intention and the plants' magick, you can even add some crystal chips, which are just as effective as full-size crystals for a fraction of the price. But if you want to skip the crystals, a simple sigil drawn on the outside of the container works wonders all on its own.

YOU'LL NEED:

- Stones or rocks
- Clear quartz chips (optional)
- Salt (optional)
- Permanent marker
- 3 large glass jars (24 ounces or larger)

- Healthy soil or potting mix
- Poultry blend fresh herbs:
  - Thyme for strength
  - Sage for cleansing
  - Rosemary for focus
- Water

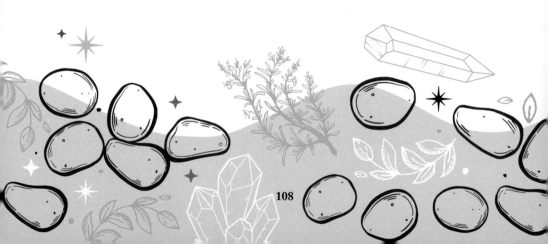

1. Boil the stones or rocks until they are clean. If you're using the crystal chips, charge them in a bowl of salt overnight. (Don't worry—a little leftover salt won't hurt the plants.)

2. The next day, set your intention to amplify the herbs' magickal properties. You can phrase this any way that resonates with you.

3. With that intention in mind, use the marker to draw a sigil on each jar. (If you're not into sigils, you can write the words "strength," "cleansing," and "focus" instead.)

4. Holding your intention, gently add a handful of stones and crystal chips (if using) to the bottom of each prepared jar. Then fill the jars with soil to within an inch or two of the rims.

5. Plant one herb in each jar, covering the roots completely with soil, and lightly water it. Then move your finished garden to a sunny windowsill to soak up empowering solar vibes.

6. Finish things off with a little enchantment by saying aloud: *May these herbs nourish and empower my energy. So mote it be.*

Hot Tip

Don't forget to shower your garden with good intentions and water alike while it grows. The vibes can be constant, but be careful not to over-water. Know the specific water requirements of the herbs you've planted. For good magickal measure, you can even use moon water (see page 170).

*Sometimes
the simplest
witchcraft is the
most effective.*

CHAPTER 5

Kitchen Witchery

Cooking Is Magick

You don't have to be a great cook to be a witch. You don't have to cook at all, actually, to be a witch (just ask some of my occult aunties about that). Maybe you use your oven to store back issues of *Vogue* because take-out makes more sense for your life than cooking. Or maybe you just don't have time very often to cook. There's nothing at all wrong with that! But there's a lot of magick to be found in the kitchen for those who are willing to stir things up. And if you do love to cook and bake, you probably have a lot of powerful ingredients on hand.

Cooking is alchemy; it's transformative. Think about how you are able to take some milk, flour, sugar, eggs, and butter and turn it all into perfect little pancakes. And every ingredient offers its own magickal properties. In other words, cooking is magick. (Literally, in Ancient Greece, where the words for "cook" and "priest" were the same: *mageiros*, meaning magick.) What can't you accomplish as witch if you harness that power for your craft?

In most modern homes, the kitchen is considered the hearth, whether you have an actual fireplace or a toaster oven. It's a source of warmth and coziness as well as a place of nourishment. All the best stories are told in the kitchen. And what's more magickal than hanging out in a kitchen with friends, drinking something refreshing and talking while a delicious meal cooks? Even if the only recipe you know is the one for your morning smoothie, you can still infuse the experience with some intention.

WORTH *your* SALT

Now that so many different kinds of salt are used in home cooking, it's much easier (and cheaper) to obtain a wide variety for your practice. And each one brings something unique to the table.

- **Table salt:** This is the food equivalent of clear quartz crystal. It can be used for any cleansing, banishing, or purification spellwork.

- **Black lava salt:** Known for its volcanic properties, you can use this salt to keep undesirable people and influences away from your home.

- **Smoked salt:** The type of wood the salt was smoked with will affect its magickal properties (hickory adds strength, for example), but, generally, smoked salt is good for protection spells.

- **Pink Himalayan salt:** Associated with love for its color, you can use Himalayan salt to break love spells, end toxic relationships of all kinds, and protect the home.

- **Kosher salt:** Blessed by a rabbi, kosher salt can be used to quickly draw out negativity.

- **Sea salt:** Because it comes from the sea, it also contains water's elemental properties. This makes it perfect for releasing emotional baggage.

- **Fleur de sel:** This is sea salt, but more delicate, and it's ideal for consecration use.

- **Gray salt:** Naturally gray, this salt is a good fit for grounding.

- **Bonus: Epsom salt:** This one's not actually a salt, but it's incredibly useful for magickal baths and floor washes. Just don't add it to your food!

Handwashing Ritual

Most of us pay a lot more attention to handwashing today than we did in years past. It goes without saying that you need to wash your hands before you cook food, but even this simple act can be infused with intention that will, in turn, infuse anything that follows. You can use regular old table salt in this cleansing ritual, or you can choose one that matches your intention. But the key is focusing on washing any negative vibes down the drain with it. Even the color of your hand towel can match your intention (red for love, pink for self-love, yellow for joy, green for abundance, and so on). Adding some lemon to this rite gives you more of everything good, and if you want a double dose, use lemon-scented soap.

This ritual can work with any intention—not just cooking-related ones. Sure, it could be as simple as, *I want this food to nourish myself and my household.* But if it's been a long day, it might be something like, *I want all of the bad vibes from angry clients to go down the drain so I can start fresh again.* You could set an intention for focus, energy, healing (yourself or others), or pretty much anything else you want. And you can set a different intention every day, or even every time you're washing your hands to prepare food. It's as versatile as it is easy and inexpensive.

YOU'LL NEED:

- Salt for cleansing
- A lemon wedge for joy, purification, beauty, and abundance
- A clean kitchen towel
- Hand soap

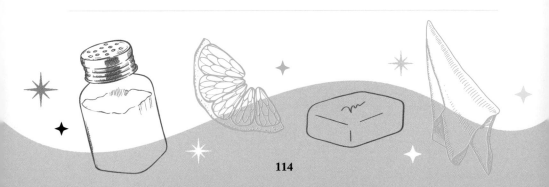

1. Choose and hold your intention, then put a pinch of salt into your hand. Squeeze some fresh lemon onto the salt.

2. Continue focusing on your intention as you rub the salt and lemon into your hands. Bring your hands up to your nose and breathe in the refreshing scent.

3. Rinse your hands with warm water. Focus on the salt dissolving as it goes down the drain.

4. Wash your hands with soap and warm water, focusing on the suds (and any residual negativity) going down the drain with the water.

5. Turn off the faucet and use the towel to dry your hands while saying to yourself: *And so it is!*

Recipes for Magick

With all the hustle and bustle in daily life, it can be difficult to make time for the actual practice part of your witchcraft. Does that mean you should just accept a life full of non-magickal drudgery? Of course not. Finding the sacred in everyday life is important in your journey of getting to know yourself as a witch. And in everyday life, you have to eat, just like you have to sleep and shower (two acts also packed with magickal potential—see pages 142 and 184). Maybe you love to make elaborate meals, or maybe shoving an apple in your maw before you leave the house is a victory. No matter how simple or elaborate you may prefer to make things, there's room to add a little magick.

As long as you're whipping something up, you may as well infuse it with intention. Maybe you need a confidence boost, maybe you want a little extra romance with your meal, or maybe you want to feel good in your skin. Guess what? All of that can be accomplished in the kitchen. The recipes in this book are ready-made for magick. Use them as a jumping-off point until you get the hang of incorporating kitchen witchery into your practice. (Who knows—maybe a few of them will become lifelong favorites.) And once you get into the habit, you'll start seeing the potential in every ingredient. That will help you buy and consume more mindfully. And if you already love to cook or bake, you'll just be making the most of the ingredients you have on hand.

When making these recipes, try to hold your intention in your mind. Consider the properties of the ingredients you're using and sprinkle them in how you imagine a seasoned witch making an amazing potion would. The care you take in presenting nourishment to yourself and consuming it honors all that's sacred within you and the Universe.

SUBSTITUTIONS, PLEASE

There's a little something here for everyone in these recipes, but you can tweak them for your dietary restrictions and preferences. As you've hopefully been learning, you can always find alternatives to components. And vegan ingredients can hold the same power as their animal-based counterparts.

Bright Start Mini Muffins

A delicious and energizing way to start your day, these mini muffins will set you up for success with just a few bites.

- 1½ cups old-fashioned rolled oats for prosperity
- ½ teaspoon baking powder
- 1 tablespoon almond butter for wisdom
- 2 tablespoons mini chocolate chips for love in all its forms
- 1 teaspoon cinnamon for success
- ½ teaspoon sea salt for grounding
- 2 large eggs, beaten, for healing
- 1 ripe banana, mashed, for luck
- ¼ cup milk (oat milk for comfort, almond milk for insight, or cow's milk for protection)
- 1 tablespoon olive oil for glamour
- 3 tablespoons honey or maple syrup to attract good vibes
- 1 teaspoon vanilla extract to regain your energy

Preheat your oven to 350°F. Mix all the dry ingredients together in a large bowl, and the wet ingredients in another bowl. Stir the wet ingredients into the dry ingredients just until combined, being careful not to overmix the batter. Let the batter rest for 10 minutes. Fill the cups of a 6-well mini-muffin tin ¾ full with the batter. Bake for 25 minutes or until a toothpick comes out cleanly. Yields 6 mini muffins.

MINI MUFFIN VARIATIONS

If you're a fan of the Bright Start Mini Muffins, you're going to love these alternatives. Just omit the almond butter, mini chocolate chips, banana, and cinnamon, add the ingredients listed here instead, and follow the same instructions.

Loving Rose Cardamom Muffins

- 3 tablespoons rose water for connection
- 3 tablespoons culinary-grade rose petals for love
- 1 teaspoon cardamom for passion

Glamourous Chocolate Pomegranate Muffins

- 3 tablespoons cocoa powder for beauty
- 3 tablespoons mini chocolate chips for confidence
- 3 tablespoons pomegranate arils for vitality

Grounding Savory Breakfast Muffins

- Additional ½ teaspoon salt for grounding
- 1 tablespoon Italian seasoning (oregano, basil, sage, thyme) for protection and centering
- 2 tablespoons Parmesan cheese for positive vibes

Bougie Blood-Orange Cranberry Muffins

- Juice of ½ large blood orange + 1 tablespoon zest for prosperity
- 3 tablespoons dried cranberries for abundance
- ½ teaspoon ground nutmeg for financial stability

Low-Key Lavender Lemon Muffins

- Half a lemon, juiced + 1 tablespoon zest for removing negative vibes
- 3 tablespoons culinary-grade dried lavender buds for serenity
- ½ teaspoon dried thyme for healing

Hit the Ground Running Breakfast Bowl

This tiny feast has everything you need to banish negativity, bring you luck, boost your security and confidence, and make you feel great.

- 1 large egg, prepared however you like it, for cleansing
- ½ large avocado, sliced, for enhancing your glamour
- 1 large tomato, diced, for protection against the evil eye
- ¼ cup chopped parsley for prosperity
- 1 cup chopped kale for increasing your power in divination
- ¼ cup favorite cheese for positive vibes
- A drizzle of olive oil for security at home and in your career
- Salt, to taste, for grounding
- Pepper, to taste, for motivation

Arrange the bowl in whatever way is visually pleasing to you. That's it! Yields 1 serving.

Empowering Chickpea Lunch Bowl

Bring this healthy, filling bowl to work in a lunch-sized container to help sustain your spirit and get you through the day. As you make it, know that you are taking in these nutrients to empower your body, mind, and spirit.

- 1 (7.75-ounce) can chickpeas, rinsed and drained, for luck
- 1 cup arugula for abundance
- ¼ cup chopped hazelnuts, for protection against the evil eye
- ¼ cup chopped dill, for concentration
- ¼ cup chopped parsley, for wealth
- 1 large hard-boiled egg, chopped, for healing
- ¼ cup favorite cheese for joy
- ¼ cup favorite cooked rice for maintaining prosperity
- Salt, to taste, for grounding and centering
- Lemon juice, to taste, for joy
- A drizzle of olive oil for empowerment

Arrange your bowl with loving intention. Yields 1 serving.

On-the-Go Charcuterie Box

Pack all of this goodness into a lunch box, and you can enjoy a centering snack anytime you need it.

- 4 sprigs fresh rosemary for knowledge
- ¼ cup favorite cheese for bliss
- ¼ cup grape tomatoes for shielding yourself against gossip
- ¼ cup favorite olives for glamour empowerment
- ¼ cup cashews for harmony
- 5 dried figs for self-love
- Freshly baked bread for grounding
- Small container honey for passion

Using the rosemary as skewers, thread on the cheese, tomatoes, and olives, then mindfully arrange your lunch box. Yields 1 serving.

Self-Love Chocolate Bark

If you need an excuse to pamper yourself, this is it. This chocolate bark is so simple to make and leaves you feeling loved and cared for.

- 9 ounces good-quality baking chocolate, chopped, for self-love
- 1 tablespoon rose water for passion
- ½ teaspoon salt for centering
- 2 tablespoons culinary-grade rose petals for self-confidence
- ¼ cup shelled and chopped pistachios for balance

Line a baking sheet with parchment paper. Add the chocolate to a saucepan over low heat and stir in the rose water. Stir constantly until the chocolate is glossy and fully melted. Pour the chocolate onto the prepared baking sheet and use a spatula to smooth it out evenly. Sprinkle the salt, rose petals, and pistachios onto the chocolate. Refrigerate overnight. The next day, break the hardened chocolate into pieces with your hands or a kitchen mallet, then peel the pieces off the parchment. Yields 10 servings.

Glam Cauliflower Tahini Steaks with Baked Sweet Potatoes

Get centered in your glamour vibes with this bit of weeknight luxury to nourish the skin you're in. You'll need to let all this goodness marinate overnight, so plan accordingly.

- Olive oil, to taste, for prosperity
- ¼ cup tahini for luck
- Juice of 1 lemon for joy
- 1 teaspoon paprika for vitality
- Salt, to taste, for grounding
- 1 head cauliflower, sliced into 2-inch-thick steaks, for manifesting your glamour

- 4 medium sweet potatoes for love in all its forms
- ¼ cup unsalted butter for tenacity
- 3 tablespoons honey for attraction
- ½ teaspoon smoked salt for grounding

Mix together the olive oil, tahini, lemon, paprika, and salt in a large container or zip-top bag. Add the cauliflower, seal the container, and leave it in the refrigerator overnight to marinate. The next day, preheat the oven to 350°F. Poke holes in the sweet potatoes and add them to a baking sheet lined with aluminum foil. Bake until tender, 1 to 1½ hours. In a small bowl, mix together the butter and honey until smooth. About 30 minutes before the potatoes are finished, move the cauliflower steaks to another foil-lined baking sheet and add them to the oven. When everything is fork-tender, remove the baking sheets from the oven and serve, topping the sweet potatoes with the honey butter and smoked salt. Yields 4 servings.

Simmer Pot Potions

Sometimes the simplest witchcraft is the most effective. Simmer pots allow you to stir up a cauldron full of magick to infuse your home with intention, *and* they are a great way to use up pricey produce and other perishables that would otherwise go to waste. These are basically intentionally crafted potions that you allow to simmer on the stove and fill your house with scent and energy (i.e., magickal potpourri). And scent is a powerful tool for witches. People are scientifically wired to associate memories and emotions with smells. Certain aromas have the power to make us feel certain ways. And that's exactly why businesses use it to sell us stuff—like the upscale hotel lobby that actually smells luxurious, or a home-decor store that smells warm and homey.

You can do more than resist their well-targeted temptations—you can harness the power of scent for yourself. What emotions do you want to evoke, in both yourself and the guests you invite to your home? Do it with simmer pots.

To make a simmer pot, focus on your intention for the mood you want to set. Add your ingredients to a medium saucepan, then fill the pan with warm water so that it is three-quarters full. Bring the simmer pot to a simmer over medium heat, then reduce the heat to low. Then just enjoy the aroma and energy wafting through your home as your intention manifests.

You'll also want to periodically check on the pot to make sure there's enough liquid to keep the ingredients from burning, adding more liquid as needed to keep the good vibes going. (And *never* leave the house with a simmer pot on the stove.) When you are finished, shut the heat off and let the pot and its ingredients cool completely before disposing of them.

Here are some simmer-pot recipes to try out, but don't be afraid to get creative. Using what you've learned so far, play with combinations based on what you want to accomplish (and, of course, how you want your home to smell).

When you're finished with a spell, you can dispose of biodegradable ingredients outside (in the woods or a compost pile, for example) as an offering to your local land and nature spirits. If that's not possible, simply thank the ingredients for the use of their energy and throw them away.

Love Is in the Air

This combination of fruit, spice, and flowers is sure to put anyone in the mood for romance. But rather than hunt down dried hibiscus, you can add the contents of a couple of hibiscus tea bags.

- ½ a fresh pomegranate, 1 tablespoon frozen pomegranate seeds, or ¼ cup pomegranate juice for beauty, vitality, and abundance
- 7 cardamom pods for passion
- ¼ cup rose petals (fresh or dried) for love in all its forms
- ¼ cup rose water for love in all its forms
- 2 tablespoons dried hibiscus for passion and liberation
- Water to fill

Kiss and Make Up

This brew works for all manner of relationships, not just romantic ones. As in the previous recipe, you can use the contents of a few lemon-balm tea bags to finish this blend.

- 1 apple, diced, for healing
- 3 bay leaves for cleansing
- ¼ cup cedar chips for purification
- 3 cinnamon sticks for quick healing
- 3 tablespoons dried lemon balm for love in all its forms
- Water to fill

Everything Is Under Control

This is a potion you want to have in your back pocket for when things start to feel like they're spiraling. Take a few deep, centering breaths over it as it simmers.

- 1 teaspoon vanilla extract for regaining control over financial matters
- ¼ cup chicory coffee for control over the situation

- 3 whole allspice pods for luck
- 3 cinnamon sticks to speed things up
- Water to fill

Chill the Tea

Sometimes you just need to relax. This calming blend relies on inexpensive teas (the kind you usually have on hand because you reach for the caffeinated stuff instead).

- The contents of 6 chamomile-lavender tea bags for stress-relief
- The contents of 6 hibiscus tea bags to prevent disagreements

- 1 bunch fresh mint for open communication
- Juice of 1 lime for calm
- Water to fill

WFH

This all-natural boost will have you feeling your best when your bed keeps beckoning you away from your computer. If you don't have fresh herbs, a sprinkling of dried will do.

- Juice of 1 orange for abundance
- 1 bunch rosemary for concentration
- 1 bunch thyme for strength and courage

- 3 pods star anise for communication
- Water to fill

This Is My Happy Place

This upbeat blend will cleanse your home of any negative or stuffy energy and leave bliss in its place. It's an especially welcoming recipe for guests.

- Juice of 1 blood orange for joy and cheer
- 1 bunch oregano for energy
- 7 cardamom pods for loyalty
- ¼ cup dried lavender for good vibes
- Water to fill

Getting Hygge with It

This simmer pot gives you all the warmth and coziness of a well-loved home without the sticker shock of a shopping trip for more home decor. In fact, it may actually attract money to you.

- Juice of 1 lemon for prosperity
- Juice of 1 orange for happiness
- 3 cinnamon sticks for success
- 1 whole nutmeg for luck
- 3 allspice berries for determination
- 1 small piece ginger root for new adventures
- Water to fill

I'm Rich, Witch!

Feeling a little overextended? This brew is for you. If acorns aren't in season (or foraging isn't on your to-do list), you can use hazelnuts instead.

- 1 bunch basil for wealth
- 1 whole head garlic for protecting your assets
- 3 acorns for wisdom
- 1 bunch parsley to attract money
- 1 bunch white sage to remove negative vibes
- Water to fill

Confidence Booster

Who couldn't use a confidence boost now and then? The lemon in this blend is not only cheery, it also helps remove any negative gunk taking up residence in your home.

- 1 bunch tarragon for self-confidence
- 7 cherries for happiness
- Juice of 1 lemon for removing blockages
- 3 tablespoons dried chamomile for success
- 7 cloves for self-love
- Water to fill

Feeling Cute Today

Confidence and self-love aren't always the same thing. This brew gives you a bit of both so you feel extra ready to face the world.

- 7 dried figs for love and prosperity
- 3 tablespoons rose water for self-love
- 7 cardamom pods for passion
- 3 tablespoons honey for attraction
- 3 chili peppers for warding off the evil eye
- Water to fill

More Potions and Elixirs

As a little kid, did you like making magickal potions using glitter and glue, or collecting rocks, acorns, and twigs for mystical rituals? This section is for you! Potions and elixirs are a great way to mix it up at home with your witchcraft. When you think about potions and elixirs, you might think about Halloween cauldrons and bottles filled with mysterious liquids. It's all in spooky fun, but, historically, people didn't always know what they were ingesting or putting on their skin. So there really was an air of mystery about medicinal products. When you make your own potions and elixirs at home, though, you'll know exactly what you're ingesting and why it works. That's a pretty fair trade for the lack of enigmatic aura. Here is a small selection of powerful and potable potions and elixirs that you can make with inexpensive items from the grocery store.

DOCTOR'S ORDERS

A lot of what makes witchcraft work comes down to science. They go hand in hand. And that's exactly why you should always talk to your healthcare provider about potential potion ingredients before ingesting anything.

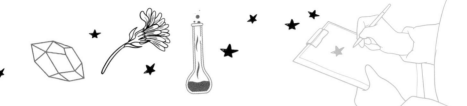

Soothing Sleepy Moon Milk

When you're having trouble sleeping, and chamomile tea isn't cutting it, this elixir can help. The energy of each ingredient combines to put you under its sleepy spell, but the valerian root doesn't hurt. It's a bit of a splurge but should last you awhile. Just talk to your doctor before trying it. And do not drive after drinking this.

- 1 cup milk (oat milk for comfort, almond milk for insight, cow's milk for protection)
- ½ teaspoon vanilla extract for restoring your energy
- ½ dropper valerian tincture for sound sleep
- 1 teaspoon culinary-grade dried lavender buds for calm
- 1 teaspoon ground cardamom for love in all its forms
- 1 teaspoon dried chamomile for removing negative vibes
- Honey, to taste, for healing

Two hours before bed, set your intention for a restorative, restful night's sleep. Add the ingredients to a small pot and bring them to a simmer over medium heat. Pour the mixture through a strainer into a mug, then stir in the valerian tincture. As you drink the moon milk, say: *I pour my will into this moon milk. May my path to sleep be as smooth as silk. So let it be.*

Heart-Healing Herbal Tea

Everyone goes through breakups, disagreements, and misunderstandings, but this potion is the perfect way to soothe those heartbreaks and start to heal.

- 1 tablespoon rose water for self-love
- Honey, to taste, for healing
- 3 tablespoons culinary-grade dried rose petals for soothing
- 3 sprigs rosemary for wisdom

Set your intention to heal your bruised heart. Add the rose water and honey to a mug. Place the rosemary and rose petals in a muslin or reusable tea bag and add it to the mug. Carefully add boiling water to the mug and let the tea steep for three minutes before removing the bag. While drinking the tea, visualize your heart beginning to mend.

Keep Calm and Drink Herbal Tea

This tea will not only help you relax but possibly also cure what ails you, whether that's an upset stomach or finicky skin. But the key is to breathe it in before enjoying it.

- 1 bunch fresh mint for prosperity and digestion
- Juice of ½ lemon for joy and clear skin
- 1 piece ginger root for soothing heartburn

- 3 pieces of star anise for warding off the evil eye and strengthening the immune system
- 1 cup water
- Honey, to taste, for healing and quelling anxiety

Center yourself in your intention. Add everything but the honey to a small pot and bring it to a boil over medium-high heat. Then shut off the stove and, using your hands, waft the steam to your solar-plexus chakra (between your ribs) to release the stress. Carefully strain the tea into a mug and stir in the honey. Leave the contents of the strainer outside as an offering, if possible, or discard them. Inhale the scent of the tea, focus on your breathing, and then sip mindfully.

Bad Day, Go Away Ginger Lemon Syrup

This elixir couldn't be simpler to whip up, but it has a powerful cheering energy. A spoonful a day will keep the bad vibes away. You can add it to tea (or cocktails) or just enjoy a spoonful directly.

- Juice of 1 large lemon for joy
- 1 piece ginger root, grated, for success

- 1 cup honey for happiness

Focus on your intention while you prepare the ingredients, then add them to a blender and blend them on high until smooth. Keep the mixture in a sealed glass jar in the refrigerator for up to two weeks.

Chakra-Balancing Herbal Tea

When your chakras are balanced, everything flows much easier, in both your witchcraft and your day-to-day life. This elixir will help you be in tune with pleasure, peace, wisdom, love, your voice, your intuition, and your awareness.

- 1 piece ginger root for your root chakra
- 1 tablespoon dried hibiscus for your sacral chakra
- ½ a lemon, juiced for your solar-plexus chakra
- 1 tablespoon culinary-grade rose petals for your heart chakra
- 1 tablespoon dried chamomile for your throat chakra
- 1 tablespoon mint for your third-eye chakra
- 1 tablespoon culinary-grade dried lavender for your crown chakra

Focus on your intention to align your chakras while adding all the ingredients to a muslin or reusable tea bag. Carefully add boiling water to a mug, then add the bag. If you feel like any particular chakras are blocked, waft the steam over those chakras. Let the tea steep for four minutes and then remove the bag. As you drink your tea, say: *May this tea balance my chakras so that I can receive their teachings. So let it be.*

Prosperity Solar Iced Tea

You'll need a hot summer day with plenty of sunshine to activate this potion, but it's worth the wait. Every sip brings you closer to success and abundance.

- 1 bunch mint for abundance
- 8 bags Earl Grey tea for success and removing negative vibes
- 1 gallon water
- Sunshine for acquiring wealth
- Lemon juice, to taste, for prosperity
- Honey, to taste, for attracting money
- Ice

Focus on your intention to acquire prosperity. Add the mint, tea bags, and water to a large pitcher and cover it before putting it outside (or on a windowsill) in the sun. Let the tea steep for 4 hours, until it achieves a rich color, then bring it inside and remove the tea bags and mint. Stir in lemon and honey before enjoying the tea over ice. Refrigerate the pitcher.

Spicy Hot Cocoa

Turn up the heat for your spicy night in. Do you want to feel sexy in your own skin? Do you want to heat things up? This elixir takes ordinary hot chocolate to the next level to add passion and romance to any evening. (And even the cheapest mix will taste gourmet.)

- 1 cup whole milk for adding richness to your love life
- Favorite hot cocoa mix
- 1 teaspoon mini chocolate chips for passion
- 1 teaspoon cinnamon for keeping things spicy
- 1 tablespoon rose water for love in all its forms

- 1 tablespoon culinary-grade dried rose petals for glamour activation
- ¼ teaspoon smoked salt for staying grounded
- ¼ teaspoon smoked cayenne pepper for warding off the evil eye
- ½ teaspoon vanilla extract for luxurious experiences

Focus on your intention while adding the milk to a saucepan. Bring it to a simmer on medium-low heat, but don't let it boil. Stir in the other ingredients clockwise while focusing on your intention and let the mixture simmer for 5 minutes. Carefully pour your upgraded hot chocolate into a mug and enjoy!

The Universe will
communicate with
you in ways that
you, personally,
will understand.

CHAPTER 6
Divination DIY

Take the Wheel (of Fortune)

Divination has existed as long as witches have, which is to say, about as long as humans have. While we've come a long way, with so much knowledge accessible to us, there are always going to be aspects of life that are difficult to read. *Where is my career heading? What decision should I make? Are all my friends mad at me?* Divination (the practice of gaining knowledge by magickal means) can be used to get a deeper understanding of a situation, to look at a situation from a different angle, and to see what your subconscious knows that your conscious brain doesn't. The best part is that you don't need a lot of "stuff" to do it. For a lot of it—from listening to your inner voice to interpreting your dreams—you don't need anything at all. (But if you're diving into divination, a deck of Tarot cards is definitely splurge-worthy.)

Steering the Ship

Divination isn't the Universe telling you what's going to happen or what to do. It's just a way to see a little more of the big picture so you can make informed decisions. The practice gives you an opportunity to steer your ship. If your divination tells you you're on the right path, you can choose to stay the course. If your divination indicates that a rough patch is coming, you can batten down the hatches or make different choices to try to mitigate the damage.

It's going to take you a little while to tune in when the Universe is sending you information out in the wild—through dreams and signs and other ways—but you will eventually be able to pick up what the Universe is putting down. Will it always make sense in the moment? Probably not! Will it often make more sense in hindsight? Absolutely! And that's how you learn what to look out for in the future. Over time, you'll hone your craft.

Is divination completely accurate all the time? Well, are weather reports completely accurate all the time? Nope. Divination, just like the weather, is based on shifting influences that are constantly changing, making 100-percent accuracy impossible. That said, the weather report is *often* correct and it *rarely* hurts you to wear boots on a day it's supposed to snow. Same with divination.

Relax, It's Just Fate

As much as we like to think things are fated or meant to be, not much is set in stone. As you get more practiced in divination, you will come to find that some events are more changeable than others. Sometimes you'll be able to change your ship's course; sometimes you won't. The part that a lot of people (including some witches) get caught up in is the dreaded "bad reading," where you intuit something alarming or pull all the worst cards and think life as you know it will go down in flames. First, there's no such thing as a bad reading. Even if you pulled every crap card in the deck, there's nothing stopping you from pulling cards until you get some positive cards that will guide you out of a negative situation. Things might be rough for a short time, but it's super unlikely that the rest of your life will be a persistent dumpster fire—just like it's super unlikely that the rest of your life will be nothing but rainbows and unicorns.

There will always be good and bad. Divination is about seeing both and making informed decisions. You will learn to consider the multiple possibilities in a reading. For example, in Tarot, pulling the Death card doesn't usually signify actual physical death. It could mean death of a relationship or death of a career. But it *also* means upheaval. So, technically, puppies, babies, weddings, and other fun things that cause a lot of chaos would fall under this card's realm.

GETTING BACK *to the* GOOD PARTS

Classically, the goddess Fortuna rules over matters of fate. She has a wheel she's always turning, and that wheel is divided into four parts: *regnabo* (I shall reign), *regno* (I reign), *regnavi* (I have reigned), and *sum sine regno* (I have no kingdom). No one is excited about the scary parts of the wheel, but seeing them in your divination can indicate a time for shadow work. Your shadow is the part of yourself you try to repress—it's usually home to your trauma and baggage. Doing shadow work means looking inward and doing the work to heal. This includes learning those hard-won lessons and dealing with personal growth that you didn't ask for but that will be useful later. When you do the work, you can figure out how to keep the wheel spinning so you get back to the good parts.

Flip a Coin Divination Practice

Make this game of chance a bit more intuitive with a magickal spin. Yes-or-no questions are a great starting point for divination. Asking questions that you already know the answers to will help you align your coin to your energy. Once your coin is in tune with you, you can start asking yes-or-no questions that you *don't* know the answers to. Record the answers and see how accurate they turn out to be.

YOU'LL NEED:

- A coin
- A piece of paper
- A pen or pencil

DO THIS:

1. Decide which side of the coin will indicate "yes" and which side will be "no." Then center yourself by taking some deep breaths.

2. Start by asking questions you know the answers to, flipping the coin each time. *Do I live at [your address]? Is my name [not your name]? Was my first pet's name [your pet's name]?*

3. Once the coin is aligned with your energy (it gets the right answer more often than not), write down questions you *don't* know the answers to and record the coin's answers. As life catches up, look back on your questions. What is your accuracy rate?

Hot Tip

If this practice isn't very accurate, don't worry! Not every divination tool works for every witch. Practice will help you determine which ones work best for you.

Little Omens Everywhere

Omens are little signs that the Universe gives us about our future. The key word here is *little*. These are just peeks into the Universe's sock drawer to see what is coming up next. It drops these almost imperceptible clues along your path as a way for you to connect with it and maybe, hopefully, steer your ship better. But because these breadcrumbs are easy to miss, you have to train yourself to see them. You do that by honing your intuition and practicing your craft.

Divination Traditions

Even if you come from generations of scientists, you probably have at least a few folk-magick traditions within your family. Maybe you break the wishbone at every Thanksgiving, pick up pennies, make wishes on dandelions, throw spilled salt over your shoulder, or knock on wood. Just like those habits, divination rituals tend to get passed down from person to person. Think about how your family does divination. Maybe your mom has particularly prescient dreams, or your aunt relies on vibes. Or maybe your grandmother was a witch herself who taught you how to scry (use an object to tell the future) and read palms. Spend some time thinking about these traditions within your family or local culture. Are you noticing more of these folkloric aspects in your day-to-day life? Can you incorporate any of these traditions into your witchcraft? The magick that's passed down can sometimes be the strongest, so traditions can be a great place to start your divination journey. The more natural a practice is to you, the easier it may be for you to spot the Universe's response to it.

Speaking the Universe's Language

Generally speaking, the Universe will communicate with you in ways that you, personally, will understand. If you see the world very visually, you will likely get visual omens, like suddenly seeing lots of fat sparrows (a symbol of joy and protection), noticing specific shapes in the clouds, or having realistic dreams. If you are more of an auditory witch, you may hear uncommon words being said in unexpected places or a particular song being repeated. You will eventually discover your own private dialect between yourself and the Universe—it just requires time and patience.

Here's one exercise that can help you hone your observational skills: When you speak to the Universe by sending out your intention, give the Universe an opportunity to speak back. Ask for it to be specific. Tell it where you'll be looking for your answer or sign. Give it a specific symbol to use for a specific meaning. (This will also take some practice.)

And remember, omens are *very* subjective. For me, seeing a feisty lobster in the tank at the grocery store's seafood counter may mean that I'm entering a very prosperous part of Fortuna's Wheel. For you, it could mean being upset by the actions of others. Neither interpretation is incorrect; it's just that different witches have different values.

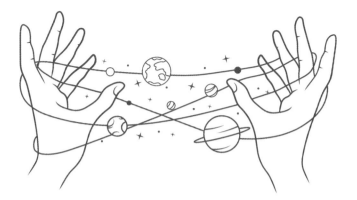

Find the Thread Communication Ritual

This spell will help you open your spirit to communicating with the Universe. For many of us, the idea of two-way communication with the Universe can sound terrifying or impossible. But don't worry—it's highly unlikely that you are suddenly going to become Joan of Arc, with angels bossily telling you what to do or getting you burned at the stake. It's much more likely that the Universe will communicate with you about smaller aspects of your day-to-day life, like telling you to think before you respond to a text. The following ritual uses a muslin bag, but you can use whatever little receptacle you have on hand. You can also add a sigil to the bag (or whatever you use) for added magickal oomph.

YOU'LL NEED:

- 1 yard of white yarn for clarity
- Sage essential oil for divination
- Moonstone for intuition
- Dried rosemary for knowledge
- A muslin bag
- A piece of paper
- A pen or pencil

1. Take three deep, centering breaths. Put the yarn in your hands and connect with your intention: to understand how the Universe communicates with you.

2. While focusing on your intention, tie seven knots in the yarn (the number seven is associated with spiritual connection).

3. Dab the yarn with the sage essential oil and say: *I open the path to receiving the Universe's wisdom.*

4. Add the yarn, moonstone, and rosemary to the muslin bag.

5. When you feel like you need guidance from the Universe about a specific issue, untie a knot and observe. The answer could be in your dreams, in songs that you hear, in plants and animals in your neighborhood, or somewhere in your travels.

6. When you get your answer, write down what it was and where you found it. Look for patterns. As you untie the knots, you should develop a clearer understanding of how you communicate with the Universe.

7. When you untie the last knot, thank the yarn for its work and discard it. (Just don't leave it outside as an offering—it can injure wildlife.)

Doing Magick in Your Sleep

You have to sleep sometime—ideally, on a regular basis for boring, human-related reasons. But it's also easier to focus your will for magick if you're well rested. Besides the fact that sleep is a mandatory and magick-boosting activity, it's also an exciting and no-cost opportunity for you as a witch. Sleep magick—and, more specifically, dream magick—is a powerful part of any practice.

Dreaming has long been considered a magickal practice. The Talmud in 1500 BCE, the Hindu Vedas in 500 CE, and Shakespeare's works in the late 1500s and early 1600s all talked about the importance of dreams. That's a lot of historical precedence to draw from. And for good reason. Through dreams, you can start to figure out what's going on with your subconscious and tap into your intuition. You can also look for hidden omens and signs of prophecy, do healing work for yourself, create spells, and find inspiration in your dreams.

The After-Dark Breakdown

Most of the dreams you'll have aren't terribly important. They aren't the stuff of prophetic visions; they're just a subconscious rerun of your day-to-day life—only with more stress, or maybe some horses running around in the background. The first step in your sleep-magick journey is learning how to tell the difference between those reruns and a dream that could actually be important in your witchcraft.

- **STRESS AND RECURRING DREAMS:** These are the dreams that make you wake up in a cold sweat. Think: your teeth falling out, being unprepared for an event, being late for something, and other anxiety-inducing things like that. This is just your brain on blender mode from the day's activities.

- **REGULAR DREAMS:** The average dream is more of the brain on salad-spinner mode, but with less anxiety. You'll probably be doing something completely normal but with a couple of quirky aspects. Just because there are fish flying over your head doesn't mean the dream is magickal.

- **NIGHTMARES:** These are scarier than stress dreams—think being chased, drowning, falling, being trapped, or even dying. If the nightmare in question doesn't have anything to do with transformation, and it's just a mix of fears or phobias, it's probably not magickal.

- **MYSTICAL DREAMS:** These rare, otherworldly dreams are more vivid and memorable than the garden-variety ones. These dreams feel important, both when you are dreaming and when you wake up. You are usually doing something action oriented in these dreams, like trying to help someone, learning something new, exploring a place you've never been, or being entrusted with a secret.

Mystical dreams are where all the exciting magick lives. Spirits, ancestors, and goddesses will speak to you here. You'll start to create your own dreamscape of places you can visit and where you can be visited. Within them, you can do witchcraft or healing work, see omens, and receive instructions about what to do in your waking life. Mystical dreams can be scary sometimes. (Being torn apart and put back together isn't uncommon.) But the good news is, you won't have many of these dreams until you get more practiced in sleep magick. And, by then, you'll know how to handle the odd prophetic spider.

GET to KNOW the REAL YOU

If a dream is a wish your heart makes, it's obviously an important aspect to your magickal practice. For one, dreams are free—not just for Cinderella (also broke), but for you too. While the hows and whys on the importance of dreams vary culturally, there's an underlying thread that's fairly universal: dreams are outside of your waking life. In her dreams, Cinderella could escape scrubbing her fingers down to the bone and forget about the snarky thing her stepsisters said and be who she actually is. The same goes for you too. Who are you? The answer will change with age and circumstance, but your dreams give you a chance to explore that primal question without consequences. Learning the answer to that question will shape your witchcraft, and your dreams could be the key.

Find the Pattern: Dream Journaling

Dreams, like divination, are often about seeing the patterns. Learning to interpret them, break them down, lean into them, and change them will impact your waking life too. Your subconscious will remind you about things your waking self may have missed or things you are trying to ignore because it's uncomfortable to deal with them. Keeping a dream journal will help you identify the patterns in your sleeping life, leading to clues for managing your waking life better.

But that can be easier said than done sometimes. Have you ever tried to remember a dream you had the night before and come up blank? You have a better chance of remembering more if you write it down as soon as you wake up. So keep a journal right next your bed, and make a habit of writing in it first thing each morning. Try to remember and write down as much detail as possible. Ask yourself questions like: Who was in my dream? What was I doing? How did I feel? Write it down in your dream diary for future reference.

Once you've recorded what you remember, think about how your dream was different from your waking life. Why do you think your subconscious has you exploring these aspects? Next, consider what aspects of your dream are the same as your waking life—outfits you own, a room in your home, a person who is special to you, plotlines and themes from something you've been watching or reading. Why do you think your subconscious has put these things in your dream life? Write it all down.

When you've written everything you can think of, look for patterns. Do you have recurring dreams? What could they be symbolizing? You can always check dream dictionaries on the internet for common themes, but your dreams' meanings could be very specific to you. If you're constantly dreaming about bears, it could mean someone in your life is un*bear*able. Or it could mean you're ready to stand up for yourself. Whatever the meaning is for you, keep track of it in your dream journal.

As you go through your day, consider how your dreams may be influencing your waking life. Are you feeling anxious because someone died in your dreams? Remind yourself that the person is alive and well (and that, in some cultures, dreaming about someone's death is actually good luck for that person). Do you feel extra confident because you punched a shark in the snout in your dream? Maybe that's your subconscious's way of telling you today's the day to ask for a raise at work. At the end of the day, write down what you think your dreams were telling you and why. The more information you have, the easier it will be to interpret your dreams, now and in the future.

Fresh Start Bedroom Cleansing

This bedroom-cleansing ritual is just what you need to clear out all the vibes that are no longer serving you so you can get some restful—and potentially magickal—sleep. It uses fresh air, clean sheets, and a steamy, simmering cauldron (slow cooker) filled with herbs made for mystical dreaming to create a positive environment for your dream work. Internal clutter can be prohibitive to mystical dreaming, so this ritual helps clear any unhelpful energy from the room for a magickally good night's sleep. **Note:** You'll need to clear a heat-safe surface in your bedroom for your cauldron and follow safety guidelines for its use. Remember, your cauldron is going to get hot. Use potholders and common sense.

YOU'LL NEED:

- 1 cup water
- Your cauldron (small slow cooker)
- Your favorite bed linens
- Laundry detergent (lavender is ideal)
- A washing machine
- Dried herbs:
  - Lavender for calm and peace
  - Rose petals for love in all its forms
  - Chamomile for sleep and accomplishment
- Fresh herbs:
  - Bay leaves for success
  - Sage for cleansing
  - Rosemary for cleansing and to keep away nightmares

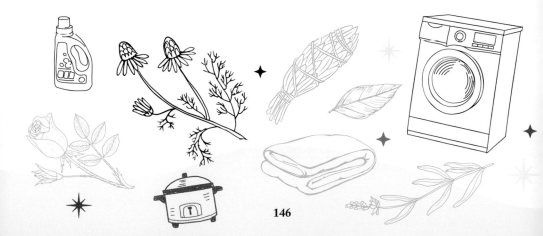

DO THIS:

1. Add the water to your cauldron and turn it to high.

2. While the water warms, focus on your intention to wash away any negative energy and put your bed linens in the washing machine.

3. Place your hands over the laundry detergent in the cap and think about everything you want to bring to your bed: restful nights, good dreams, growing dreamscapes, and so on. Add the detergent to the machine and wash your linens as usual.

4. When you take the bed linens out of the washing machine, breathe them in deeply while holding your intention. Then dry them as usual. (Fresh air and sunlight can add another layer of energetic cleansing, but a dryer is fine.)

5. Place your freshly laundered linens on your bed and open any windows in your bedroom. All those negative vibes you washed out of your linens? Visualize any stragglers leaving through the windows, then close them.

6. While focusing on your intention, carefully add your herbs to the cauldron. (A pinch of each will do.)

7. Make your bed with your freshly cleansed linens, then lie in it for at least ten minutes while focusing on your intention and inhaling the scent of the herbs beginning to simmer. When you're done, place your hands at least 6 inches above the cauldron and carefully bring the scented steam to your face so that you're bathed in your intention. Then shut off your cauldron and thank it for its work. Once the water has cooled completely, you can leave the mixture outside as an offering or simply thank it and discard it.

Learning How to Swing (A Pendulum)

Learning to use a pendulum is the next step in your divination journey. A pendulum is a small weight (often a crystal) suspended by a length of chain or thread, which you hold to allow the weight to move freely. The idea is that you hold the top of the chain, and the pendulum points you toward the answers you seek. These magickal tools have been used for almost as long as there have been humans and witches, and there are all different kinds. Some people believe that pendulums move of their own accord, but, really, it's our own subtle reflexes moving them. You can look at it as your subconscious being in charge of your body's reflexes, trying to give messages to your conscious brain. In addition to being incredibly insightful, using a pendulum is also an affordable way to dip your toes further into divination.

Making Your Own Pendulum and Board

Most often, you'll use some version of a pendulum board in this practice. It's similar to using a Ouija board, as the pendulum sweeps over letters and phrases to answer your questions. (Only it doesn't touch the board.) And although you can find beautiful, handcrafted boards for a price, you can simply print one of the many templates available online or sketch your own. It doesn't need to be fancy to be effective. Some boards include letters and numbers, but one with just "yes" and "no" is perfect for beginners.

Elaborately decorated crystal pendulums are also hard to pass up but unnecessary. Instead, you can use 1 yard of thread in whatever color you think will be best for the work, the essential oil of your choice, and a small screw-eye hook from the hardware store (1 inch or smaller) as the weight. Thread your strand through the screw eye so that you have even amounts of thread on either side. Focus on your intention (to use this pendulum for divination) as you tie three knots at the top of the eye. Then tie the ends together using three more knots. Put your new pendulum in a small bowl with salt on a windowsill to charge in the moonlight overnight. (You should cleanse your pendulum like this every so often too.)

Pendulum Basics

Just as you did with the coin-flip ritual on page 137, you'll start attuning your pendulum to yourself and the board by asking it yes-or-no questions that you know the answers to. You don't need a board just yet. Pinch the top of the thread in your dominant hand and rest that elbow on a table. Give the pendulum a tap with your non-dominant hand to set it in motion, then focus on your question. If the pendulum spins clockwise, that means *yes*. If the pendulum spins counterclockwise, that means *no*. But don't force it—just let your energy do the work. Once you have the pendulum attuned to your vibes and it's answering questions correctly (for the most part), you can start using a board and asking more complex questions.

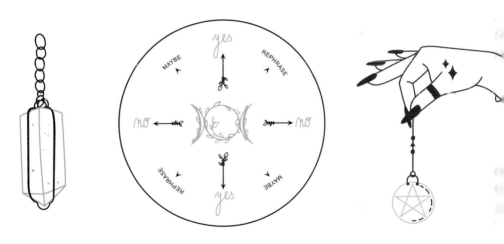

BOOST YOUR SIGNAL

If you have them, you can place crystals around the board to amplify your intention. You might use rose quartz for questions about love and friendship, amethyst for clarity, citrine for finances and career, clear quartz to amplify any question, or some combination of those crystals. You can also dab the pendulum itself with an essential oil blend of three drops of frankincense (for spiritual connection), three drops of patchouli (for attunement), and three drops of orange (for success).

Pendulum Test Drive

Now that you have attuned your pendulum to your vibes and the board, it's time to take it for a real test drive. This ritual couldn't be simpler, but it can be extremely informative. You can ask questions like: *Is this the right career path for me? Am I focusing on the right career goal for myself? Is this romantic relationship right for me? What lesson do I need to learn from this friend? What do I need to learn as a witch?* But, remember, divination isn't black and white. You may not always get answers to your questions. And even when you do, you'll need to interpret them. That, in and of itself, takes practice.

YOU'LL NEED:

- Crystals aligned with your intention (optional)
- An essential-oil blend aligned with your intention
- A tealight
- A pendulum
- A pendulum board

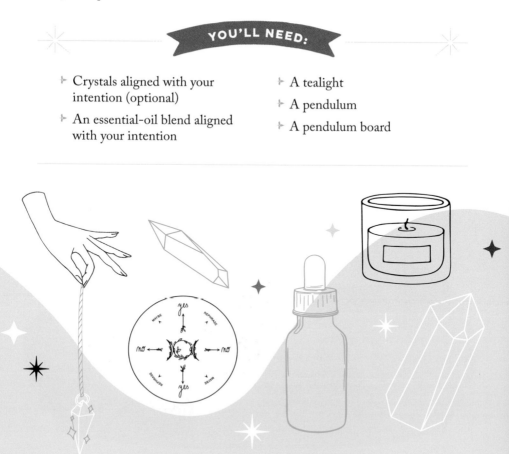

1. Take a few deep, centering breaths. If using crystals, place them on or around your board.

2. Dab a little of the essential-oil blend over your third eye (the spot on your brow that sits between your eyes) while focusing on your question.

3. Add three drops of the blend to the tealight and light it.

4. With the end of the chain or cord between your index finger and thumb, hold the pendulum over the board, ask your question and set the pendulum in motion.

5. Watch the pendulum and notice whether it begins to swing toward or hover over a particular letter or phrase. (You can also check your interpretations by holding the pendulum over the letter or phrase and asking for confirmation.)

6. When you're finished, say thank you and goodbye to end the session.

Hot Tip

Keep a journal of all your readings so that you can learn from your questions, answers, and interpretations. Over time, you'll notice patterns and begin to speak the Universe's language more fluently.

Tarot 101

Another magickal object that is worth the splurge is a deck of Tarot cards. And, as splurges go, these decks are usually on the low end of the spectrum. Once you've bought the cards, the practice itself is free. Tarot can help you gain perspective and clarity about specific questions and future forecasts. Plus, it's just a fun addition to your witchy repertoire. When you've gotten comfortable reading for yourself, you can even expand your skills and read for others. (But that, like all things, takes time, patience, and practice.)

MORE *to the* STORY

Tarot is a nuanced and fascinating practice that dates back to the fifteenth century, which is why you can find a treasure trove of books on the subject. (And plenty of them are at your local library.) The following is a basic overview, but the practice is certainly worth a deeper dive.

Choosing a Deck

Some people believe that your first Tarot deck should come as a gift. But that's a lot like waiting around for someone to buy you flowers when you can go outside and pick them yourself. You want to work with a deck that resonates with you. Thankfully, there are many to choose from, with varying levels and styles of decoration and instruction. Choose a deck that you enjoy, because you'll be working with it a lot to get it attuned to you.

Respecting the Energy

Working with the cards every day will help them align with your energy and make your readings more accurate. But even just shuffling the deck and sleeping with it under your pillow can be helpful. When you are not actively using the cards, keep them in a Tarot bag or a piece of fabric so they aren't soaking up random energy. When you feel they need a refresh, you can charge your cards in a bowl of salt on a windowsill overnight. You can also keep a piece of clear quartz in the bag with them.

Working with the Cards

You will find no shortage of interpretations online for each card, and that's a good (and free) place to start. But it's also good to really *look* at the cards. What images or words pop out at you? Why? What feelings do you get when you look at each individual card? Why? Keeping a journal of your impressions and readings can help your readings become more consistent. Although there are standard interpretations, your unique perspectives and experiences add to them. Over time, you'll develop your own relationship with the cards.

TAROT *to* GO

In some parts of South Korea, it's not unusual to see Tarot trucks, which are like food trucks that serve up prophecies instead of tacos to people stumbling out of clubs late at night. Tarot trucks are popular after clubbing for the same reason comfort food is. The night feels full of fun and possibility. Will every Tarot-truck reader be able to correctly predict every *soju*-fueled dance sesh's future? Of course not. But if the reader tells you to be wary of new acquaintances, it's not a bad idea to take a closer look at that new crush.

The One-Card
Tarot Reading

There are a number of spreads or layouts that you can work with in readings. A three-card spread can give you a peek into the past, present, and future. The Celtic Cross spread can give you a big-picture overview of a sticky situation. But the simple one-card reading is a great place to start and build your skills. You can add crystals, oils, and sigils aligned with your intention to the ritual, but all you really need is your Tarot deck and a few quiet minutes. The more you practice, the more your deck will become attuned to you.

YOU'LL NEED:

- Your Tarot deck
- A journal or piece of paper
- A pen or pencil

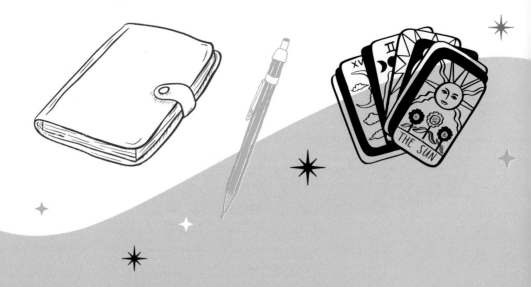

1. Take three deep, centering breaths. Focus on your question: *What do I need to know about my day?*

2. Shuffle your cards until it feels right to stop. Be patient—it takes as long as it takes.

3. Decide whether you want to cut the deck or just pull a card from the top, then lay your card face-up in front of you. Before you look up its meaning, consider what words and images seem important to *you* and how that card makes you feel. Write it down.

4. Look up the meaning of the card and write down what you get from it.

5. Before bed, reflect on the day and consider how it proves or changes your interpretation. Write that down too.

Hot Tip

**Some people choose to read the opposite meaning
into cards that appear upside-down ("reversed"),
while others read the card the same either way.
You can do whichever feels right to you.**

This is your sanctuary—you get to decide who and what has access.

CHAPTER 7

In Your Defense

Safety First

When doing any kind of magick, you need to protect your energy—from outside influences, from inner chaos, and even from magickal mishaps. Your energy is arguably the most important factor in your witchcraft. It feeds off your mind, body, heart, and environment, and it influences the outcome of everything you do, both practically and magickally. Anything you can do to help keep yourself safe and protect your energy, you should do. And there is a *lot* you can do.

THE EVIL EYE

If you've been in the witchy world for more than five minutes, you've probably heard of the evil eye and seen the amulets from many cultures meant to ward it off. (The blue eye is a popular one.) The evil eye is a type of magickal curse designed to cause harm to something or someone. But, more often than not, it's cast by ordinary, not-terrible people who don't even know they're casting it in a moment of envy. You may not know who cast it or why, but if you feel like you're having a run of bad luck, it never hurts to protect against it. (You can learn how on page 183.)

Tiny Bag of Protection Charm

If you feel like you need a little extra witchy protection for whatever reason—warding off negative energy on an important day, keeping annoying people out of your hair, etc.—this little charm bag can help. It'll be most effective if you keep it close to you (in your pocket or purse, for example), but you can also keep it in your car, at your desk, or wherever else you need a little extra defense.

YOU'LL NEED:

- A tealight
- A small muslin bag
- Frankincense essential oil for protection

- A sigil aligned with your intention
- 1 teaspoon salt for protection
- 1 bag peppermint tea for protection
- 1 hematite stone for protection

DO THIS:

1. Anoint the candle and the bag with three drops of frankincense each.

2. Light the tealight while focusing on your intention to be protected.

3. Charge each magickal component by breathing your intention onto them.

4. Add the components to the bag, then carefully run the bag over the tealight while saying: *May I be safe. May I be protected. May I be formidable. So mote it be.*

Protecting You from Yourself

Being able to control your emotions—especially when stressed—is an important part of energetic self-defense. And you already know how to do it. The things you've learned in this book and through your practice can help you navigate tricky situations in life and magick so you can protect your energy from the everyday stuff that can get under your skin.

All witches are human first, so we have to put up with garbage on occasion just like everyone else. What witchcraft can do is deepen your understanding of your shadow self, remove the evil eye, and help you work through healing yourself. When you start to get into ritual work and setting intentions, you'll quickly get to the heart of what you want for yourself and your life, as well as what's standing in the way of it. This self-discovery will help you grow into your witchcraft even more than herbs and crystals will. (And introspection is always free—or, at least, inexpensive.)

Check Your Compass

When someone else's energy is messing with yours, or you're in an emotionally fraught situation (like a breakup or coven drama), you need to put a little distance between yourself and that negativity to be effective in your witchcraft. It sounds so easy when it's abstract. *We're no longer serving each other, so we shouldn't invest time and energy in each other.* Simple, clean, sensible. It's a lot different when your emotions are involved, receipts are being pulled, and other people are involving themselves. This is *always* a good time to come back to your moral compass as a witch. Look back on what you wrote about it and ask yourself how you can align with that energy again. Give yourself a night to sleep on it. See what dreams come to you and whether you feel more centered in the morning.

Rise Above

We all get wound up sometimes—being a witch doesn't make you immune to that. And a good venting session doesn't always help. That's because those heated thoughts, feelings, and actions that you expressed can reinforce your own negative self-talk. Does that mean you should vow never ever to be catty or gossipy ever again? You could, but it's unlikely to stick. (Because, again, human.) What you *can* do is work to reduce the time you are spending engaged in those behaviors. Part of how you can do that is by taking a step back when emotions are running high to ground and center yourself as a witch. (See page 32.) Coming back to your craft and the focus you've cultivated can help you sail on top of murky waters instead of sinking.

Protecting Yourself from Others

The sad truth is that, sometimes, people will intentionally try to cause you harm. But, as with the evil eye, most harm is unintentional (or at least not intended maliciously). One of the perks of being a witch is being able to protect yourself from all of it. But how you choose to protect yourself can have consequences of its own. Shielding yourself and returning negative energy are both good options. Even the light jinx can work. But the point of protecting yourself is to shield your energy, not hurt people back. (Keep that in mind when you're tempted to throw a hex at any particularly toxic exes.)

Shielding

If you are in a situation where you feel like someone is throwing a lot of negative energy your way, you always have the option to shield yourself from it. This creates an energetic barrier that keeps you safe from less-than-amicable magickal influences. To shield yourself, imagine drawing a protective circle around yourself. Think about how safe it feels inside of that circle and the protection it offers. If you are wearing a protection charm of any kind, touch it. When you do, say: *I call upon the Universe to shield and protect me from harm. Please hear my call and keep me safe.*

Weaponized Kindness

Kindness doesn't seem like it would be protective against negative influences, but it can be if you use it right. We're not talking about *niceness*, which is generally performative. Niceness is easy to fake. Kindness is often unseen and can be difficult (especially when using it toward someone who's upset you) because it has to be sincere. Thankfully, there's incentive: kindness is often a pebble in the shoe of your opponent because they're not getting the reaction they want or expect. They might even think you're plotting something—which you are. You are plotting to be kind. How very devious of you. And almost against their will, they will feel more positively inclined toward you. Genius. But the best part is that your energy gets an instant lift too.

To wield kindness magickally, take time in your day to wish this other person well by sending positive vibes their way. Again, for it to be effective, it has to be sincere, and it may take some time for you to get to that place. Focus on an intention you genuinely mean. You may not like or forgive this person, but you can choose to respect them and wish them well (or at least not wish them ill). You could also bake them something with this intention, use positive affirmations (compliments) on them, or offer them your genuine energetic support. But you *should* also set firm boundaries when interacting with them, magickally and emotionally.

Hexes

Witchcraft will not solve every problem you ever have. Hexes will not only *not* solve your problems, they will also likely create a few of their own. These kinds of spells often end up energetically tying you to the person you are attempting to punish, which just creates a bigger dumpster fire. Hexing is also often discouraged for new witches because learning the scale and scope you need to wield this magick responsibly takes years of experience. And you know what's hard to do when you are feeling a lot of feelings? Making responsible decisions in witchcraft and your day-to-day life. But introspection, grounding and centering, shadow work, divination, and taking a few days to cool down are always good (and free!) options.

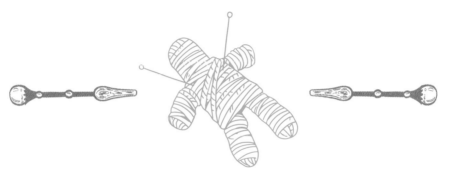

YOU'RE ONLY HUMAN

Sometimes, pettiness sings its siren song to us. The trick is to make sure you won't wake up one day full of regret. Generally, pinching back when pinched doesn't trigger a regretful response. But if you escalate from pinching back to setting the other person's lawn on fire (metaphorically speaking, of course), you will likely have regrets. So don't do that. Instead, stick to pinching or, better yet, rising above. You can't afford to start any metaphorical lawn fires anyway.

A Ritual for Cutting Ties

All your witchy introspection may have helped you realize there is a relationship (or two or three . . .) in your life that isn't serving you anymore. Maybe at one time it did, maybe you've raised your standards, or maybe you have difficulty letting go. All of those are valid reasons to have lingered a bit too long in a relationship. But acknowledging that those ties are no longer serving you is the first step in claiming your power for yourself as a witch.

Cutting ties isn't just to keep this former relationship away from you, it's also to call your own energy back to yourself. All that time and effort you put into that relationship? That's energy given. It was yours to begin with, and there's no reason you can't reclaim that power for yourself now. This will give you more energy (literally) to pursue opportunities with people on your current wavelength. Best of all, it's a simple spell that uses very few components.

YOU'LL NEED:

- A tealight
- Lemon essential oil for moving someone out of your life
- Scrap paper
- A pen
- Salt for banishing

- A small knife
- 1 whole lemon
- A piece of cheesecloth large enough to wrap the lemon
- A piece of cotton twine
- Lemon juice

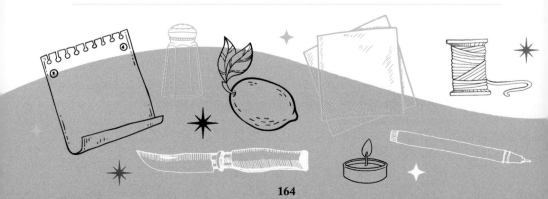

164

1. Take a deep breath and center yourself. Anoint the tealight with the lemon oil, then light it with the intention to cut ties with this person and reclaim your own energy.

2. On the paper, write down your reasons for cutting ties with this person.

3. Add a pinch of salt to the paper and fold it away from yourself three times. Cut a small slit in the lemon and slip the paper into it.

4. Wrap the lemon in cheesecloth and twine, like it's a gift. Once the tealight has burned out, take the lemon to the nearest public dumpster or trash can. Focus on reclaiming your own energy as you gently throw the lemon over your left shoulder into the trash receptacle and walk away without looking back.

5. When you get home, wash your hands with soap, salt, and some fresh lemon juice. Say: *I have reclaimed my own energy. So let it be.*

Mirror, Mirror (A Return-to-Sender Spell)

A return-to-sender spell is exactly what it sounds like: sending negative energy back to its source. Is it the nicest thing to do? Nope. Would they have anything to worry about if they weren't sending all that negativity your way in the first place? They would not. It's up to you to decide whether this practice aligns with your moral compass. But if you choose to perform it, do so during a waning moon, which helps you banish bad vibes.

YOU'LL NEED:

- A small compact with a mirror
- A dry-erase or glass marker
- A sigil aligned with your intention
- Sage essential oil for banishing negativity
- Lavender essential oil for your inner peace
- Lemon essential oil for releasing the other person's negativity

DO THIS:

1. Take a deep, centering breath. Focus on your intention that this mirror will act as a ward against negative energy.

2. Use the marker to sketch the sigil onto the mirror and close the compact.

3. Continuing to hold your intention, put one drop of each essential oil on the outside of the compact. Once dry, carry the compact with you.

4. If someone is sending negativity your way, calmly and discreetly take out your compact and flash the mirror toward them (ideally without them seeing it) while saying to yourself: *I'm not a dumpster for your negative energy. I'm not holding this for you. Take it right back. Return to sender.*

5. Renew your intention and re-anoint the compact with the three drops of oil during each new moon.

A Gossip-Stopping Goody Bag

If you've been the subject of someone's gossip lately, and you'd like it to stop, this may be the ritual for you. This is witchcraft that requires working your will over someone else. You want this person (or persons) to stop gossiping about you, and it's safe to say that they *want* to gossip about you. That means you are putting your desire above theirs. (The same is true in most spells involving other people, especially love spells.) If you are OK with that, proceed and keep the charm bag close to you whenever you are going to see the gossiper(s). But if your moral compass doesn't point in that particular direction, there's no shame in sticking with shielding.

YOU'LL NEED:

- Salt to banish negative vibes
- 3 cloves to stop gossip
- A packet of sugar to sweeten the gossiper toward you
- Amethyst for calm
- Hematite to soak up negative vibes
- A clear quartz crystal to amplify your intention
- Sage oil to banish negativity
- A small scrap of paper with the name(s) of the gossiper(s) on it
- A muslin bag
- A tealight

DO THIS:

1. Take a deep, centering breath. Hold all of the components in your hands and focus on your intention that these people stop gossiping about you. Breathe your intention onto them. Anoint the tealight with three drops of sage oil.

2. Light the tealight and add the rest of the components to the bag. Carefully pass the bag over the tealight's flame three times.

3. Say: *I command you, [name], to stop gossiping about me. So let it be.*

Protecting Your Space

Now that you know how to protect yourself, what about your space? Whether it's your room or your entire home, you want that space to be a safe space for yourself and a sanctuary as much as possible. That means checking negative vibes at the door, inviting in luck and abundance, and keeping the energy clear and receptive. Warding your home is a low-cost way to do all this plus deepen your connection to your hearth and strengthen your magick.

Positive Vibes Only?

It's easy to assume that making your home a sanctuary means keeping all negative vibes out of your space. But you know where negative vibes come from sometimes? Yeah, you. Also partners and friends who you likely want to visit your home. And you know what's normal? Bad days, work stress, and squabbles. You know what's not normal? Constant positivity. Leave a little space for the normal ebb and flow of life in your home's magickal protection system. You don't want to accidentally magickally lock yourself out of the house on a bad day.

Normal levels of negativity can be cleared with a simmer pot and some open windows, both of which are really simple and inexpensive solutions. (See the Fresh Start Bedroom Cleansing Ritual on page 146.) Does that mean you have to fling open your door to unfriendly exes, family members with awful opinions, and frenemies? Of course not. This is your sanctuary—you get to decide who and what has access. (And you'll need a lot more than a simmer pot to get Brad's narcissistic vibes out of your space.)

Two magickal ingredients you're probably going to come across in your practice are moon water and Florida water. Moon water is exactly what it sounds like: water that's been charged by the moon. Waxing-moon or full-moon water can be used for manifestation; new-moon or waning-moon water can be used for banishing. As long as you have a jar, tap water, and a windowsill, moon water is free. Florida water is a spiritually charged (and alcohol-based) cologne full of powerful oils that's been around since 1835, and most grocery stores offer it inexpensively (sometimes in the hair care aisle). Many witches use it in spells and hearth-cleansing rituals.

Warding Your Home

An important aspect of shielding and warding your home is keeping your home clean—magickally speaking. Open the windows to let negative vibes out. Simmer cleansing ingredients like lemon, rosemary, and cedar chips regularly. Use an inexpensive cinnamon broom to sweep negative energy out the door. (Make sure you get the closets!) Wipe down your windowsills, doorways, and mirrors with Florida water or moon water. Keep cleansing crystals (like selenite or black tourmaline) over your doors.

In addition to cleansing your home, you'll want to work on keeping the bad stuff out and drawing some good stuff in. From horseshoes to hamsas, you can find plenty of other protective amulets to use around your home. And the same cinnamon broom you use to sweep out negative vibes can hang on the wall by your door for good luck. You can also draw protective sigils under the doormat with sidewalk chalk, sprinkle salt and rosemary over thresholds for warding off negative energy, or blow a bit of ground cinnamon across thresholds to attract abundance. All these rituals and practices combine to create the witchy sanctuary of your dreams. (Skip spilling ingredients on the floor if you have pets, though. With all the good energy they contribute, they deserve a safe space too!)

Charge It Up
Full-Moon Ritual

A full moon is an excellent time to make moon water, which will supercharge any witchcraft you use it for. You can use it to boost a cleansing bath, to cleanse your magickal components, to water your plants, to anoint your body, to cleanse your altar, or to remove negative energy from any space in your home. Although you don't need much to make moon water, this ritual can take things up a notch.

YOU'LL NEED:

- A clear quartz crystal or chips for clarity
- A moonstone crystal or chips for new beginnings
- A selenite crystal or chips to raise your vibes
- A pinch of salt for charging

- A little rose water for love in all its forms
- A clean glass jar with a lid
- Water that has been boiled and cooled

DO THIS:

1. On the night of a full moon, add the crystals, salt, and rose water to the jar while focusing on manifesting your intention to create moon water that will be used to supercharge your witchcraft.

2. Breathe your intention into the jar, then add the water and seal the jar with the lid.

3. Place the jar on a windowsill overnight to charge in the moonlight. Say: *I bless this water to be sanctified by the light of the moon. So I will it, so it is.*

A Spell Jar for Warding Your Home

Even something as simple as a spell jar can help you safeguard your sacred space. Crafted with intention and carefully chosen ingredients, this one becomes a potent shield for your home. You'll place it by your front door so it can act as a sentry, warding off unwanted influences and even overzealous protections. (Remember, you only want to keep out the things you never, ever want in your home, like dangerous or draining energies. Don't unintentionally lock your own energy out of your space.)

YOU'LL NEED:

- Frankincense incense for defense and consecration
- Amethyst for protection
- Salt for banishing
- A small scoop of dirt from your yard or where you live
- Lavender for peace
- Rosemary for binding and protection
- Clear quartz crystal for amplification
- Hematite for shielding
- A small ball of tinfoil for protection
- A small piece of paper inscribed with a sigil aligned with your intention
- A small jar with a lid

DO THIS:

1. Light your incense and set your intention to ward your home.

2. Waft some of the incense smoke over your components and into your jar.

3. Add the components to the jar in whatever way feels right to you.

4. Breathe your intention into the jar and seal it.

5. Either bury the jar just outside your front door or keep it inside by your door.

It's a deep fire
within you built
on confidence,
self-love, and
self-worth.

CHAPTER 8

Modern Glamour Magick

I Love That for You

Contrary to popular belief (and television), glamour magick isn't some kind of witchy disguise or mind game wherein people see only what you want them to see. Glamour magick is about boosting your confidence and being the best version of yourself. And when you present that high-vibe version to the world and to yourself, the world often responds positively. (That's the goal, anyway.) You can use crystals, oils, amulets, and all kinds of magickal components to help you achieve your glamour, but you can also use the cosmetics you already own—or even just a bit of introspection. That makes glamour magick one very broke-witch-friendly practice.

It's Not What You Buy

Our culture tends to commodify glamour just like it commodifies witchcraft. We're constantly being sold "miracle" products that promise to make us beautiful, ageless, and desirable. And we buy them. Which is easier: working on your inner terrarium or buying a new lipstick? Right. But we are more than an impossible goal of being beautiful, ageless, and desirable, so we will need more than lipstick to find our glamour. While cosmetics can be a *part* of glamour if that speaks to your particular glamour expression, it is not the *point* of glamour. The point of glamour is to connect with what makes you *you* (which requires a bit of shadow work), not to act out a makeover montage to avoid dealing with stuff you don't want to deal with.

174

It's The Stories You Tell

If there's anything witches know how to do, it's to make something out of nearly nothing. More than that, it's to make that nearly nothing into something sacred and glamorous. We'll make a cordial from freshly grown strawberries and gifted vodka and give it a ridiculous name like Lucrezia's Lustful Lament. We will serve it in gorgeous thrifted glasses on a creaky table laden with tealights in jelly jars tied with twine. And we'll sip them over tales about local spirits who play when the moon is right. In other words, broke witches can put a magickal spin on anything. And that's exactly what you need to do to create your glamour—glamourize your personal narrative in the stories you tell yourself and others. Your own self-image is everything. Speak and act your beautiful truth into existence.

You Are a Bonfire

True glamour is more than expensive shoes, more than bottle service at the club (is that even still a thing?), and more than what others think of you. It's a deep fire within you built on confidence, self-love, and self-worth. When you are at your darkest, lowest point—like you have nothing left to give, you'll never be worthy, and you can't remember what it means to find something beautiful—that's when you go into your bathroom and turn out all the lights, stand in front of the mirror, and look for your true self reflected back. That's your glamour. That's your bonfire. And it's always burning.

LIGHT YOUR FIRE

To light that fire within you, create small rituals for yourself that help you explore your glamour. You could enjoy a luxurious bath, shower, or sauna; do some mirror work, sigil work, or journaling; or perform daily Tarot readings—whatever vibes with you as a witch. Some glamour-enhancing components that can help are rose petals, rose quartz, citrine, pink salt, the color pink, chocolate, jasmine essential oil, figs, oysters, and rose water.

175

What Is Your Glamour?

Your glamour is part of your magickal trifecta: your witchcraft, your day-to-day life, and your glamour combine to help you manifest your intention. In other words, it adds to your power as a witch. And, like witchcraft, glamour is inclusive. Everyone has glamour. It doesn't look like one thing. It doesn't require perfection. It's a magickal expression of what makes you an individual, as a witch and as a person. Figuring out what that looks like takes work, but it's worth it.

The Heart in the Darkness

Glamour is rooted in you in one of two ways: There's the glamour you build by wishing the world was different from what it actually is and wishing *you* were different from the way you actually are. And then there's the glamour built from your own personal truth, accepting the world around you as it is right now, and being aware of everything dark and bright that lives inside you. Which one do you think will be critical to your own evolution? Yeah, it's always the hard one.

Doing the shadow work to find your own personal truth is what's going to help you create your own glamour. Ask yourself the following questions. (Journaling about your answers can help too.)

- What makes you feel confident within your inner terrarium? Why?
- What aspects of yourself make you feel powerful? Why?
- Which of your physical aspects make you feel self-assured? Why?
- How does your power as a witch manifest for you?
- How does your glamour contribute to others in your life?
- How have difficult experiences transformed you?
- What's one thing you did today that makes you feel proud? Why?

This is about uncovering and harnessing your inner flame—the things that fuel you. That's your glamour. What does that look like?

Making It Real

Once you figure out what you want, you can start to figure out how to do the day-to-day work and witchcraft to get there. Practically, glamour is how you speak to the person at the deli counter, the scent you choose to wear (or not wear), how you choose to dress and present yourself in the world, when and why you choose to be particularly charming or particularly aggressive, and how you go about it. Magickally, it's the smallest pieces of your witchcraft coming together into a wall-sized tapestry, one stitch at a time—from the sigil you drew on your mirror with lipstick to the shadow work you do to strengthen your glamour.

Sometimes doing the work isn't enough to get there. Even after you stop getting in your own way. Even after you get brave and pursue the things you most desire. Even if you have help from others. Being in tune with your glamour can help you figure out what to do differently in your daily life and your witchcraft. It opens the doors to possibilities you hadn't previously considered and gives you the chance to be brave and do things that you are afraid of doing. You need that braveness in your witchcraft, and your glamour will help you find it. Don't be afraid to ask yourself, *Is this my best self?* It's impossible to be your best self at all times (you are still human). But checking in with yourself will help you cultivate your glamour so that it gels with your moral compass.

Embrace Your Inner Morticia

A fun and free exercise as a witch—especially if you are doing shadow work—is to look at those parts of yourself that you find challenging and figure out how to make them glamorous. Just look at Morticia Addams. She's taken being an outcast to a whole different level of glam in the way she speaks, the way she dresses, and the way she behaves. She's not trying to be what society wants her to be; she's embracing—nay, celebrating—herself for who she is. Maybe you wear sexy underwear when you feel down, or you take a candlelit bath after a hard day. Maybe you make yourself an extra fancy coffee at home before work. Romanticizing your life is part of your glamour, which exists in the dark within you as much as it does in the light.

Creating a Glamour Talisman

An activated talisman can act as a focus for your glamour. It will hold the energy of your intention close to you, constantly infusing you with it, as well as act as a physical touchstone or reminder of your intention. All you need is an item that you will wear or carry with you every day—a piece of jewelry you love, an essential oil blend that brings you joy, a charm that aligns with your intention, or whatever works for you.

YOU'LL NEED:

- Your talisman of choice
- A journal
- A pen or pencil

DO THIS:

1. On a Friday (the day of the week ruled by Venus), focus on what makes you glamorous while holding your talisman.

2. Lick your (clean) finger and touch it to your talisman so that the talisman is linked to your will.

3. Repeat this ritual every Friday and keep a daily journal on how your glamour is manifesting as you move through the world.

Bold Glamour

Feeling glamorous—feeling good in your own skin—is its own kind of shiny protection against the world. That's why some witches refer to cosmetics as war paint—they use them as armor. And you can too. You could set an intention for success, to attract new romance, or to feel braver.

For best results, choose your cosmetics with intention (concealer to hide your secrets, red lipstick for passion, highlighter for confidence, and so on). Color, fragrance, and formula can all impact your manifestation. Your makeup brushes are your wands. You can even draw a sigil on your wrist in perfume. Get creative! The more you get into this ritual, the better it will work.

YOU'LL NEED:

- A tealight
- Rose water for self-love
- Rose petals for self-confidence
- Cosmetics aligned with your intention
- A fragrance aligned with your intention
- A mirror
- A dry-erase or glass marker
- A sigil aligned with your intention

DO THIS:

1. Take three deep, centering breaths, and set your intention for your glamour. Anoint the tealight with the rose water and rose petals.

2. Carefully lay out your cosmetics and components in front of your mirror and light the tealight. Draw your glamour sigil onto the mirror with the marker and activate it with the rose water and your intention.

3. As you apply your makeup and fragrance, do so with intention. Focus on the cosmetics acting as a physical manifestation of your glamour. See yourself and your glamour in the mirror.

4. When you have finished applying your cosmetics, say: *I am a manifestation of my glamour. I am the spark. I am the bonfire.*

5. Let the candle burn out or extinguish it.

Invisible Glamour

Whatever your feelings toward cosmetics, you don't have to use any to create a glamour. If you don't like lipstick, or if perfume makes you break out in hives, that's fine. There are lots of invisible cosmetics you can apply, from fragrance-free moisturizer to hand sanitizer to witch-hazel toner. And they give you an opportunity to layer your intentions as well.

Choose your components with intention: organic moisturizer to feel nourished, sunscreen to protect against unwanted attention, honey-infused lip balm to sweeten your words. Everything you put on your body can add to your manifestation. Get creative!

YOU'LL NEED:

- A tealight
- Rose water for self-love
- Rose petals for self-confidence
- Invisible cosmetics aligned with your intention
- A mirror
- A sigil aligned with your intention
- A small makeup brush

DO THIS:

1. Take three deep, centering breaths, and set your intention for your glamour. Anoint the tealight with rose water and rose petals.

2. Carefully lay out your products in front of your mirror and light the tealight. Pass your makeup brush over the candle, then use the brush to draw your sigil onto yourself with more of the rose water wherever it feels right.

3. Say: *I am the fire that burns bright, the wind that moves me, the water that soothes me, the earth that grounds me. What I create, I manifest. I manifest my glamour.*

4. Extinguish the candle or let it burn out.

The Magick of Social Media

Social media is a wild ride as a witch because a lot of energy is expended there, with both good and negative vibes. And the apps can be incredibly seductive (especially the ones that don't include relatives who post disagreeable opinions in all caps). They have pretty pictures, hot gossip, and influencers who convince us that all our problems can be solved by green juice and lip gloss. But instead of spending more money on things you don't actually want, let alone need, you can use these shiny corners of the internet to your magickal advantage.

The Upside

If glamour is about presenting your best self to the world, social media is a worthy tool for the job. Trot out your best hashtags, your best 'fits, your best poses, and your best filters. This is a place for you to be the person you want the world to see. It's also a place for you to express yourself as a blossoming witch. And, best of all, scrolling and posting are totally free. (As of right now, anyway.)

The goal of glamour magick, of course, is to actually *be* your best self and not just show a glamorous façade. And, as we all know, social media is often a smokescreen, showing only the good parts of someone's life and hiding the bad. That's why you won't be using it to ignore the bad stuff. You'll face that head-on with your shadow work. But if you're still working on creating your glamour, consider your social media profile an exercise in "fake it 'til you make it."

The Downside

It can be challenging to remember that pretty much *everyone* is being selective with their social-media posts. What witch hasn't worked themselves up into a froth about someone else's so-called perfect life? But from your family and besties to your frenemies and exes, it's all a curated show. And getting caught up in that FOMO and envy can drain and dim your energy. So make sure you're curating *your* feed to inspire you and help you create the glamour of your dreams. (And maybe unfollow anyone who makes your blood boil.)

EVIL-EYE EMOJIS

Remember to include evil-eye amulets on your social profiles to help protect your energy there. It can be a picture of your amulet prominently displayed or an emoji in your bio, but make sure you're shielded, even on the internet (maybe *especially* on the internet).

The Evil Eye

When you think about the evil eye (an old-school phrase for when someone throws a lot of serious envy your way, either intentionally or unintentionally), you probably think about a witch spending a lot of time and energy concentrating on throwing it onto a specific target. While that can happen, most of the time the evil eye is thrown by someone who does not identify as a witch and doesn't mean to do it. They have a moment of hardcore envy, they throw that energy your way without even thinking about it consciously, and then they go about their day, never giving you another thought.

Social media is a breeding ground for the evil eye because it's so easy to focus on what others have and forget about the hard stuff they might not be posting. And witches aren't exempt from that. Forgetting about those balancing factors makes it really easy for you to throw the evil eye at them as well. As a witch, you need to be careful with your own envy. You don't want to be flinging the eye around with wild abandon. When you start to feel green, be present with the emotion. Then spend a little time thinking about what you really want for yourself and how you can get it.

Whether it's intentional or not, you'll know someone has given you the evil eye when you're having a harder time than usual in your day-to-day life. It could look like an irritatingly persistent physical sickness of some kind, financial problems, exhaustion, restless sleep, clumsiness, communication issues, or a run of bad luck. Luckily, there are lots of ways to deal with it (and it never hurts to try one if you suspect you're afflicted).

It's Nothing Personal Evil-Eye Removal

There's not much you can do about the evil eye getting thrown your way because the person throwing it probably doesn't even realize they are doing it. But what you *can* do is periodically take the evil eye off yourself.

YOU'LL NEED:

- Olive oil
- Water
- 3 small bowls
- A pinch of salt

DO THIS:

1. Start by checking to see if you've got the evil eye on you. Fill a small bowl with water and dribble a bit of olive oil into it. If the oil forms a shape like an eye, pour the water down the drain and proceed with the rest of the steps. If the oil does form the shape of an eye, it means you do not have the evil eye on you at this time, so you do not need to proceed with the ritual.

2. Pour about a tablespoon of olive oil into an empty bowl. Place your hands over the olive oil and say: *In the name of the Universe, I ask for the evil eye to be removed from me. I remove any negative vibes that have been thrown at my back. I reclaim my power as my own, free of the will of others.*

3. Fill the last bowl with water. Dip the little finger of your right hand into the olive oil and let three drops fall into the other bowl of fresh water. If the drops don't form eyes, the evil eye has been broken. Throw a pinch of salt over your left shoulder.

4. If the drops form eyes, repeat the process using your own words until they don't. (Make sure you use fresh water, olive oil, and bowls each time.)

Self-Care Is Glamour

Bathing is something you need to do regularly anyway, so why not make it magickal? After all, bathing rituals have been a part of spiritual practices for thousands of years. It works as a blessing, a manifestation of removing negative energy from you, and *kosmesis* (which is a fancy word for "makeover" that dates back to *The Iliad*). Everyone deserves the glamour of a lovely bathing ritual, and it works even if all you have is a small shower. You can sprinkle the tub or shower with lavender buds and rose petals, diffuse essential oils, or soak in scented Epsom salts to make bathing a glamour-enhancing ritual. You can also infuse self-care staples like face masks and body scrubs with intention and turn them into powerful glamour potions.

Brightening Strawberry Face Mask

This gentle face mask will not only make your skin glow but also brighten up your glamour. In this recipe, your blender or food processor will be your cauldron.

- 10 fresh strawberries for glamour empowerment
- 3 tablespoons honey for self-love
- 1 tablespoon coconut oil for cleansing
- 1 tablespoon rose water for the love others have for you

Take a centering breath and, holding your intention, add everything to a blender. Mix until smooth. Apply the face mask to your face with intention, let it sit for 15 minutes, then rinse it off. Discard any leftover mask.

Exfoliating Lip Scrub

Sweeten your words and (gently!) slough off the past with this scrub.

- ▹ 1 tablespoon honey, gently warmed, for love in all its forms
- ▹ 1 teaspoon sugar to attract positive influences
- ▹ 1 miniature glass jar

Take a centering breath and, holding your intention, mix the honey and the sugar together in the jar. Whenever your lips need some extra TLC, or you want to sweeten the words that come through them, rub the scrub into your lips while holding your intention, then rinse it off. Keep the scrub tightly sealed and use it within one week.

Rejuvenating Body Scrub

With this simple scrub, you can reinvigorate your glamour by removing past negativity (and dead skin cells) while attuning to all the deliciously abundant energy around you.

- ▹ ½ cup coarse sea salt to remove negative vibes
- ▹ ¼ cup olive oil to attract abundance
- ▹ 4 drops orange essential oil to invigorate your energy
- ▹ 4 drops sage essential oil to remove negative vibes
- ▹ 1 small glass jar

Take a centering breath and, holding your intention to remove unwanted negativity, mix all the ingredients together in the jar. In the shower or bath, apply the scrub to wet skin in a circular motion while focusing on your intention. Keep the scrub tightly sealed and use it within one month.

At-Home Kosmesis

Kosmesis is a sacred art used by Greek goddesses to take back their power. While you can always have a special, specific intention in mind during kosmesis, you can also just focus on making the everyday sacred and concentrating on how that feels to your spirit. This ritual uses the DIY recipes on pages 184 and 185 so you can connect more strongly (and inexpensively) to your witchcraft, but store-bought options are more than fine.

YOU'LL NEED:

- Candles for calming
- Exfoliating Lip Scrub
- Brightening Strawberry Face Mask
- Rejuvenating Body Scrub
- Your fluffiest towel
- A favorite face moisturizer

1. Take three deep, centering breaths, set your intention, and light the candles. Dim or turn off the lights.

2. Rub the lip scrub into your lips, concentrating on the sacredness and permeance of the words that will come from your mouth. Rinse it off.

3. Apply the face mask to your face and focus on the luminous nature of your spirit. Leave the mask on for 15 minutes as you concentrate on what you would like to manifest for yourself through kosmesis. You can do this through writing, drawing, meditating, or even a solo dance party. Then rinse it off and run a shower.

4. In the shower, apply the body scrub. Concentrate on removing negative vibes from your physical body, making sure to get the bottoms of your feet and palms of your hands. Then visualize other people's envy, past arguments, and unkind self-talk being washed down the drain.

5. When you finish showering, wrap yourself in your towel and focus on the warmth of the love that others have for you and that you have for yourself.

6. Seal the glamour in by moisturizing your face. And so it is!

Your magick
is at its most
powerful when
you feel loved,
seen, and
supported.

CHAPTER 9

The Company You Keep

Finding Your People

Are you a solitary witch, yearning for like-minded souls to share your journey? Building a coven and working together with fellow witches can be a transformative experience. And having that network of support is especially helpful for broke witches. Not only is making new friends free (minus the odd cup of coffee), knowing even a few equally thrifty witches can help you save money. Just think of what you can do when you pool your resources!

Searching for Kindred Spirits

In the digital age—especially since witchcraft is having a (hopefully very long) moment—it's easier than ever to find like-minded people. Here are a few low- or no-cost places to look:

- **ONLINE COMMUNITIES:** Join forums or social-media groups or participate in virtual gatherings and discussions and embrace the opportunity to engage with fellow practitioners from all walks of life. (Or just lurk for a while and see how it goes.)

- **LOCAL GATHERINGS:** While scrolling, keep your eyes peeled for witchy events in your area, such as workshops, meetups, classes, or even festivals. These gatherings are great places to share knowledge and discover potential coven mates who resonate with your energy.

- **WITCHY STORES:** Although you don't want to tempt yourself into overspending on shiny new things, local stores are great places to scope people out and start conversations. Plus, shops often hold free events like lectures and readings.

Sharing Is Caring

There's nothing wrong with going it alone if that's what's right for your journey. But if you find the right people, pooling magickal resources and responsibilities can lighten your load, expand your practice, and save you money. Here are a few things you can look forward to:

- **KNOWLEDGE AND WISDOM:** Within a coven, members bring their unique perspectives, expertise, and knowledge to the table. Sharing information, spells, and magickal techniques enhances everyone's learning and growth.

- **FINANCIAL BENEFITS:** By pooling resources, coven members can save money on spell ingredients, ritual tools, and witchy books. Group purchases and shared expenses make it more affordable to explore new practices and invest in pricier items.

- **SUPPORT AND ASSISTANCE:** Whether it's lending a helping hand during ritual preparations, offering guidance in spellcasting, or providing emotional support during challenging times, a coven can be a safety net that lightens the load of individual witches.

- **COLLABORATIVE SPELLWORK:** Joining forces for spellwork—love spells, protection charms, abundance rituals, or any other types of spells—amplifies your energy and intention while also strengthening the coven's bonds.

BROKE WITCH TIP

If you live in a city, it's going to be much easier to find fellow witches to connect with through witchy shops and meetups. Find your fellow witches and swap small-space tips, trade herbs, barter handmade candles for handcrafted goods, trade rooftop honey for handspun ritual cord, impart lessons you've learned about city witchcraft the hard way, and share where to find inexpensive witchcraft components. City witches can make so much from so little because so many of them love a challenge and an adventure!

Creating a Safe Space for Magick

The concept of "safe space" has been around since about ye olde 1989. It means to have either an ideological or a physical space where you feel safe to actually be yourself—a space free of emotional and physical harm such as harassment, discrimination, and abuse. For witches, it's important to have space where you can explore your identity as a witch and share your experiences without fear of repercussion. Witches don't often have dedicated spaces for their practice like many spiritualities do. It's often a borrowed space, like a clearing in the woods or someone's living room. As long as it works for you, where you create your safe space makes no difference.

What Does It Mean to Be Safe?

If you gather in a group or coven, you will not agree about everything. You can have disagreements about witchcraft, ritual start times and directions, whose turn it is to bless the cakes, and many other exciting topics that are sure to come up when working with others. What feels safe for one witch may not feel safe for you. If a safe space doesn't feel safe to you, you always have the right to leave it and discuss later (or not!) why it didn't work for you. It may be helpful for your group to have a procedure for discussing these kinds of things. It could be *Robert's Rules of Order*, a group chat, or whatever else works for everyone. But everyone in your group should feel safe to express themselves. Will it be a perfect process? Of course not—you may be witches, but you're still human. That doesn't mean you shouldn't try to create a space for your coven to feel secure.

Curating Coven Covenants

When you work as a coven (even if it's a coven of two), start by figuring out your guidelines. Considering your procedures and setting expectations can help you create a safe space from the outset. And if you decide to invite other witches, they'll understand what they are agreeing to participate in. Here are some questions for you and your founding members to consider:

- Is someone in charge? How is that person selected? How often and how will a new leader be selected? What decisions does this person make for your group?

- If your group is non-hierarchical (no leader), how are decisions made? Will you put them to a vote? Is a majority enough, or do you need consensus where everyone agrees?

- Will you follow a specific ritual format? Who leads the rituals? Do you take turns?

- How does someone new join your group? What happens if there are personality conflicts? What happens if someone feels unsafe? How and why would someone be asked to leave?

- Is initiation part of your coven structure? Are you initiated for a certain timeframe, or is it a lifetime commitment? How is education handled?

- Are there any secret parts of your coven that only coven members can know?

- If someone wants to leave the coven for whatever reason, how do you handle that?

- How are ritual components handled? Who is responsible for bringing them and buying them?

The guidelines you set may change and evolve as you do and as your coven does. Let them! Part of creating a safe space is having the freedom to grow and do better.

Although witchcraft can be serious work, there's always room for creativity when working with a group. Part of what makes creativity happen as a group is spending time together so you have a vibe. Make sure you carve out time to hang out and enjoy each other's company. It'll strengthen your bond *and* your magick.

Moon Rituals

Moon rituals are a perfect way to see how well you work together as a coven. (But they are also excellent for solo work, so don't be afraid to try them out yourself. Remember, you are the captain of your own ship.) Harnessing the power of the moon's phases can help you level up your magick, as each phase has unique energy and magickal properties. The new moon is great for new beginnings and cleansing spells, the waxing moon works well for growth and confidence, the full moon is the quartz crystal of phases—amplifying intention—and the waning moon can help you banish unwanted energy and people. Not bad for totally free magick!

It's Just a Phase New-Moon Ritual

The new moon is a great time for some shadow work, giving you the opportunity to look at parts of yourself that are hidden in your subconscious or that you find hard to face. You don't have to be afraid of your shadow self; it is a part of you just like your smile or your fingernails. We all have a shadow self. The deeper your connection is to your inner terrarium—the light parts and the dark parts—the deeper your connection to your witchcraft will be. The more you know yourself and your will, the better you will be at wielding your magick. And exploring that as a coven can help strengthen your knowledge of each other and your energetic bond. (Just decide how to divvy up the ritual's steps beforehand.)

In the darkness of the ritual, you'll consider your shadow using a few sample prompts. If other things come up for you, though, remember that this is a safe place for you to explore these parts of yourself. When you're finished with the ritual, consider journaling, sketching, or vlogging about your discoveries. Or, if you're working as a group, talk about them. Tapping into the collective can give you greater insight and support.

YOU'LL NEED:

- A small black candle (and candle holder) for breaking negative patterns
- Lavender oil for healing
- A few hematite chips for balance
- A small bowl (ideally black)
- A sprig of fresh sage for centering
- A small jar of water (moon water, if possible) for cleansing
- A timer

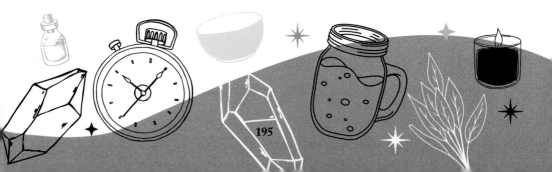

1. Go to a place in your house where it's dark—a bathroom or a closet (just make sure you have enough room to safely light a candle). Or, if you are in a group, do this ritual at night with minimal lighting wherever you usually meet.

2. Anoint the candle with lavender oil while focusing on your intention to connect with your shadow self. Light the candle.

3. Put the hematite chips in the bowl followed by the sprig of sage and a few drops of lavender oil.

4. Pour the water into the bowl, set a timer for 15 minutes, and gaze into the water by the candlelight. Consider the following questions (quietly together or aloud one at a time):
   - What emotions do I tend to avoid and why?
   - What does my inner saboteur say about me? Is any of it true? How can I be kinder to myself?
   - What makes me unkind to others? How can I work on that?

5. When the timer goes off, say: *I hold space for my shadow self. My shadow self is a part of me. Blessed be my shadow self.*

6. Sprinkle some of the water from the bowl on top of your head and leave the rest out overnight as an offering.

Making New Spiritual Besties

Some witches feel drawn to working with spirits, goddesses, and ancestors. Others may feel like this is akin to making imaginary friends that you cannot see or even understand, let alone believe exist. You may go from one viewpoint to the other. There's no right path except for the one you choose for yourself, and you're no less of a witch either way. But if it's fear or uncertainty keeping you from trying to connect with a new spiritual bestie, this section may be able to help dispel it.

About Offerings

You may have heard that spirits, goddesses, and ancestors require offerings when you work with them. But you don't need to go find a grimoire from the Middle Ages or a Holy Grail to see if you can be friends. Offerings don't need to be expensive or elaborate to be effective or to show care. In your human relationships, and as a broke witch, you don't welcome new friends into your home with the finest of caviar and expensive champagne (I hope!). A cup of tea and bread with butter and jam is more than sufficient. The same is true for any new spiritual beings you befriend. You can also make offerings to the Universe or to local nature spirits, most of which fall into the biodegradable category. When in doubt, you can never go wrong with fresh water as an offering. (And, remember, you can make offerings in your inner sanctum that are as elaborate as you would like them to be without having to worry about breaking your piggy bank.)

Take It Slow

Spiritual relationships are just like human ones. Common courtesy is always appreciated, and every spirit, ancestor, and goddess have unique preferences. You need to take your time getting to know one another. It's OK to make mistakes when you're just starting out. You'll grow and learn as you go. And even if it's a match made in heaven, you may disagree from time to time. Boundaries are important. In all exchanges, use your manners, be gracious, and be hospitable, but make sure you never, ever make any promises or vows you cannot keep for any reason. Humans don't like that, and neither do potential spiritual besties.

If you feel aligned to a particular spirit, goddess, or ancestor, you can do some research to figure out what they like and don't like, who they tend to get along with, and why. You can also just ask them what they want and wait for a sign. Once you are a little more familiar, you can start making offerings and expressing gratitude for the good things you have in your life. If you feel confident that *you* have been a good spiritual bestie, then you can ask for help. You do this through the candles you light, the witchcraft you do, the food you make, the things you offer, your shrines, your altars, the seeds you plant, and the nature you care for. With your actions, you are saying: *I am making this thing for you because I love you. Sometimes I need help. I will try not to* only *reach out when I need help. I will try to offer my time, my energy, and the things that I have to share as freely as I can.*

Just as you might not feel a connection to certain spirits, goddesses, or ancestors, not every spirit, goddess, or ancestor is going to feel a connection to you. Sometimes things start strong and fizzle out; sometimes things start more quietly and build. Generally speaking, if you ask for an omen within nine days to indicate that the potential new bestie is interested in seeing where things go, and you don't receive anything (and you've done divination about it), it may not be a match. If that's the case, you should probably stop pestering the potential new friend, just like you would any humans in your day-to-day life.

It's a Two-Way Street

Just like in human relationships, spiritual relationships go both ways. Your new spiritual bestie may also ask for things in return. And, like a human, they may not be inclined to do you any favors if you have not been a good friend. So if you ask your otherworldly friends to help you in a way that is akin to asking your human friends to help you move with only a few days' notice and vague promises of beer and pizza, they will likely expect a lot in return for that favor. And if you constantly come to either with your hand out, they may eventually feel used and mistreated and not want to do you any more favors. You are not entitled to anyone's energy, aid, or gifts, regardless of whether or not they're human.

Goddess Help Me Offering Rite

Now that you know the etiquette surrounding offerings to spirits, goddesses, and ancestors, you might be wondering how you actually do the thing. Offerings just have to come from the sincerest place in your heart. You don't need much to perform the ritual—a physical representation of your spiritual bestie (which can be a printed picture in a frame, a sketch, a sculpture, a story, or whatever works for you) and anything you think they would like. This ritual can be performed at your multipurpose altar, or you can set up a dedicated altar for the purpose.

Veneration is kind of a scary-sounding word that may make you think of getting on your hands and knees. (Some witches feel called to those levels; some don't.) It just means *deep respect*. You can venerate other humans, nature, the Universe, spirits, goddesses, and ancestors. How you express it in offering rites is up to you. It can be in words from your heart, a song, art, or the offerings themselves.

YOU'LL NEED:

- An altar cloth
- A physical representation of your spirit, goddess, or ancestor
- Physical offerings (flowers, sticks, rocks, feathers, shells, food, incense)
- A small plate or saucer
- Fresh water
- A cordial glass or other drinking glass
- A candle aligned with your bestie
- A candle snuffer
- A small firesafe bowl
- A divination tool of your choice
- A journal or grimoire
- A pen or pencil

DO THIS:

1. Arrange all your components on the altar cloth so that they are pleasing to look at, pour the water into the glass, and light the candle in the firesafe bowl.

2. Explain to your spiritual bestie what you've brought them and why, then offer them veneration (respect).

3. Take some time to be present with the spirit, goddess, or ancestor.

4. Ask for your new bestie to speak back to you through your divination. Write down anything you sense or receive.

5. When you're finished, thank your bestie for coming, extinguish the candle, and leave the offerings overnight if possible.

6. The next day, dispose of the offerings in whatever way you feel would please your bestie (or would be most environmentally friendly).

Hot Tip

If you choose to do offerings outdoors for any reason, do **not** use candles. Your spiritual bestie will not take kindly to you causing a forest fire.

It's Only Natural Offering Rite

Even if you aren't in the market for new non-corporeal besties, that doesn't mean you can't engage in offering rites and connect with the natural world and the Universe in a deeper, more meaningful way. (Yes, you can ask for favors too if you are following the previous guidelines.) Remember, more than anything, offerings come from a place of deep need—a need to connect, a need for help, a need to express gratitude. The most important part is to find a natural offering space or object that you feel connected to and have regular access to. And it doesn't have to be big—it could be part of your yard, a tree, your container garden, or even a houseplant. You may not see immediate effects from your offering, but if you keep a watchful eye out, you may be surprised by the response.

YOU'LL NEED:

- Fresh water
- A small vessel
- The divination tool of your choice
- A journal or grimoire
- A pen or pencil

DO THIS:

1. Bring the components to your offering location.

2. Make an offering of the water by saying something from your heart to consecrate it. Pour the water onto the location and offer your veneration (respect).

3. Ask for the spirit of the land, nature, or the Universe (whomever you're making the offering to) to communicate its response through your divination tool while using it. Write down anything that comes to you.

4. Thank the entity for showing up for your offering.

Mi Casa es Mi Casa

Have you ever thrown a party where you wanted to go to bed, but your guests were still happily carousing, showing no signs of leaving? You're eyeing all the half-eaten nibbles littering tabletops, the forgotten cups, and the overflowing trash can and sink, and all you can think is, "OMG! Leave! Just leave!" (Even Miss Manners basically says that you should stand up and stare at your guests until they get the hint.) Well, it's no different with spiritual besties. Think about how many sacred stories and folktales deal with the issue of hospitality and witches. In *Sleeping Beauty*, a fairy was left off the guestlist for a boring baby shower and was so irate she rained chaos over the kingdom. Things haven't gotten any less complicated in our modern witchy lives.

Make Some House Rules

Just like you probably wouldn't invite a complete stranger off the street to come live with you, you shouldn't invite spirits, goddesses, ancestors into your life until you are really sure that's what you want. Even visiting should come with a social contract. This is your sacred space. What house rules must spiritual entities follow to be invited inside your home? How are they similar to your rules for humans visiting your home in your normal life? How are they different? When you've decided on your house rules, say them out loud to your new potential spiritual bestie(s). Ask for an omen that they have accepted and plan to abide by the rules. Don't go any further until you've received that message. If they want to push your boundaries in ways that make you feel uncomfortable, you are probably not a good match for each other. Thank them for their time and energy and politely suggest they leave. If they don't take the hint, you can even use Florida water to banish their presence.

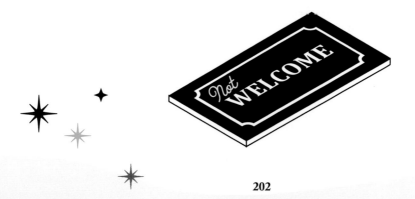

You're Still the Captain

Some of us were taught not to question authority—*especially* spiritual authority. But part of being a witch is making spiritual decisions for yourself. You can look up to others and learn from their experiences, but you will have to live with whatever choices you make. Have there been times when I wished I listened more to my occult aunties (or my mother, for that matter)? Oh, without a doubt! But I needed to learn for myself and make my own mistakes, and you do too!

Always question the motives of others—*especially* spiritual besties. What would they have to gain if you did what they asked of you? Just because someone (goddess or human) tells you to do something, it doesn't mean you should do it. You should definitely *not* do it blindly. Goddesses (and spirits and ancestors) have their own agendas. It can be thrilling to have direct contact with any of them, but you also need to be in tune with your own needs and desires. Is what you are being asked to do in service of your own agenda? Why or why not? Can you get clarification? Do you feel seen and heard? If not, then don't do it. It's that simple. It's much easier to not do something or even to wait until you feel comfortable doing something than to try to undo your actions later.

Making Beautiful Magick Together

Whether you're working with new friends or old, spiritual besties or human ones, your magick is at its most powerful when you feel loved, seen, and supported. Being a witch was never about the cottagecore aesthetic, the shiny crystal obelisks, or the massive stores of oils and potions. It's about the energy you put into it and how your practice reflects it. Focus on creating healthy, nourishing relationships with yourself and others, and you'll create beautiful magick.

Ritual Index

Magical Intention Key

Being a broke witch can mean getting creative with your spellwork. Luckily, magickal ingredients are multipurpose. Use this key when you need to swap a listed component for what you have on hand, or to create your own rituals from scratch. Your intention is what matters most.

BALANCE: hematite, pistachios, smoky quartz

CLARITY: amethyst, aquamarine, cardamom, clear quartz, lavender, mint, nutmeg, pine

CONFIDENCE AND STRENGTH: cedar, citrine, clear quartz, green aventurine, hematite, nutmeg, olives, olive oil, rose petals, rosemary, tarragon, the color orange, thyme, tiger's eye

COMMUNICATION: cardamom, honey, mint, star anise, the color yellow

COURAGE: aquamarine, cloves, ginger, hematite, oak, red pepper, the color red, thyme, tiger's eye

CREATIVITY: cardamom, citrine, lava stone, lavender, orange, rosemary, sage, smoky quartz, the color yellow, tiger's eye

GROUNDING: bread, hematite, lava stone, salt, smoky quartz

HAPPINESS: bay leaves, bergamot, cheese, cherries, citrine, jasmine, lavender, lemon

HARMONY AND PEACE: amethyst, cedar, frankincense, green aventurine, lavender, selenite, the color blue, violets, willow

HEALING: allspice, amethyst, apple, aquamarine, chamomile, clear quartz, eggs, frankincense, ginger, green aventurine, honey, lavender, rose petals, rose quartz, rosemary, selenite, the color purple, willow

INTUITION AND PSYCHIC ABILITIES: clear quartz, frankincense, jasmine, moonstone, nutmeg, star anise, violets

LOVE (IN ALL ITS FORMS): cardamom, chocolate, figs, ginger, hibiscus, honey, jasmine, lavender, lemon balm, maple, patchouli, pink candles, roses, rose hips, rose otto, rose petals, rose quartz, rose water, strawberries, sweet potato, the color pink, violets, willow

LUCK: allspice, banana, cardamom, cedar, chickpeas, ginger, green aventurine, moonstone, nutmeg, oak, star anise, tahini, the color green

MONEY, PROSPERITY, AND ABUNDANCE: allspice, arugula, basil, bergamot, cardamom, cedar, cinnamon, citrine, cranberries, figs, ginger, green aventurine, maple, mint, nutmeg, oats, olive oil, orange, parsley, patchouli, pomegranate, star anise, sunshine, the color gold, the color green, vanilla

POSITIVITY: chamomile, cheese, hematite, honey, jasmine, lemon, maple syrup, mint, orange, pine, selenite, tiger's eye, violets

PROTECTION: allspice, amethyst, basil, birch, cedar, cloves, ginger, hazelnuts, hematite, milk, mint, oak, patchouli, pine, red pepper, rosemary, sage, salt, selenite, star anise, the color black, the color purple, thyme, tiger's eye, tomato, violets

SLEEP AND DREAMS: chamomile, moonstone, nutmeg, smoky quartz, star anise, the color blue, valerian, violets

STRESS: amethyst, chamomile, lava stone, lavender, rose petals, sage, sandalwood, tiger's eye

SUCCESS: basil, bay leaves, bergamot, cedar, chamomile, citrine, ginger, moonstone, orange, the color gold, thyme

WISDOM: almonds, amethyst, aquamarine, bay leaves, rosemary, the color purple

About the Author

DEBORAH CASTELLANO is a longtime practical witch who enjoys making witchcraft accessible. She's the author of *Glamour Magic: The Witchcraft Revolution to Get What You Want* and *Magic for Troubled Times: Rituals, Recipes, and Real Talk for Witches*. When she's not writing, you can find her crafting or watching reality TV in New Jersey with her husband and their two cats. You can learn more about Deborah's work by visiting her website: www.deborahcastellano.com.